I'm Not Okay & That's Okay

Mental Health Microskills To Deal With Life's Inevitable Struggles

Steff Du Bois, PhD

16pt

Copyright Page from the Original Book

Publisher's Note

This publication is designed to provide accurate and authoritative information in regard to the subject matter covered. It is sold with the understanding that the publisher is not engaged in rendering psychological, financial, legal, or other professional services. If expert assistance or counseling is needed, the services of a competent professional should be sought.

NEW HARBINGER PUBLICATIONS is a registered trademark of New Harbinger Publications, Inc.

New Harbinger Publications is an employee-owned company.

Copyright © 2023 by Steff Du Bois
                New Harbinger Publications, Inc.
                5720 Shattuck Avenue
                Oakland, CA 94609
                www.newharbinger.com

All Rights Reserved

Acquired by Ryan Buresh; Edited by Gretel Hakanson

Library of Congress Cataloging-in-Publication Data on file

TABLE OF CONTENTS

Introduction: Nobody's Always Okay, Because Struggle Is Inevitable	vi
1: Check, Please!	1
2: Connect the Dots	4
3: Pooh-Pooh Because It's True	8
4: Tiny Interventions	12
5: TEAPOT on Repeat	16
6: Scooby-You	20
7: Time to Flex	24
8: Miss Interpretation	27
9: Do Self-Compassion	31
10: The Dud at Your Party	35
11: C You Later!	39
12: FOMO's Cousin DODI	42
13: Rewind, Be Kind	46
14: Those Annoying GNATs	49
15: Strong but Wrong	53
16: Failing Feelings	57
17: Make Conditions, Not Decisions	61
18: Be Your BFF, Not Your Bully	64
19: Put the Self in Self-Care	68
20: Thank the Crank	71
21: That's So Meta(phor)	74
22: Mirror, Mirror	77
23: Look Over There!	81
24: Set Your Alarm and Your Intention	85
25: The Blame Game	88
26: Let's Get Visual, Visual	92
27: Convert Your CDs to MP3s	96

28: You Live, You Unlearn	100
29: Create Space	104
30: Count Your ACEs	108
31: What to Do with Trauma	111
32: The WAIT-ing Game	115
33: Give Life to Your Loss	118
34: Pause for Pride with a Praise Phrase	121
35: The Challenge System	124
36: What's the Delay?	128
37: You Might Suck Too Much	131
38: Aesop in Your Brain	135
39: Manage Your E(motion)mail	139
40: Make a To-Don't List	143
41: Write a Pre-Script	146
42: Sign Your Own Permission Slip	150
43: Take an UPR	153
44: Your Should Just Got Real	156
45: The Taylor Swift Chapter	160
46: Eye Statements	164
47: The Mean-ing of Life	167
48: The Act of Faux-giveness	170
49: Name Your Nasty Thoughts	173
50: From A to ZZZ	176
51: Function and Fashion	180
52: Write the Next Chapter	183
Acknowledgments	185
References	186
Back Cover Material	196

"Steff Du Bois gives us a witty, funny, honest, and wildly helpful book of therapeutic gems that will fuel self-reflection, growth, compassion, and better mental health. Their approach is the best possible fusion of a well-trained therapist, a wise mentor, and a friend you text at midnight. We will all be better off spending some time with this glorious and insightful book."

—**Breanne Fahs,** author of *Burn It Down!* and *Women, Sex, and Madness*

"I sped through Steff Du Bois's *I'm Not Okay and That's Okay*, then went back and read it again to make sure I hadn't missed anything. Du Bois, with great empathy and deep clinical knowledge, normalizes not being okay, then gives digestible, clear, and easy-to-follow instructions on how to healthily respond to life's stressors. Du Bois's coping mechanisms and gentle guidance were revelatory."

—**Anton DiSclafani,** professor of English at Auburn University, and author of *The After Party*

"Steff Du Bois is the only person I know who could write such a smart, practical, enjoyable book about managing life's struggles. The science behind his recommendations is robust, and he makes it so clear and relatable that I think it's one of the few self-help books you cannot read without changing.... A gem of a book."

—**Gloria Balague,** president of APA Division 47 (Sport and Exercise Psychology) in 2012; and former sports psychologist for the US Track and Field Olympic Team, the US Gymnastics Olympic Team, and the Chicago Bears

"*I'm Not Okay and That's Okay* is an incredible tool for LGBTQIA+ people and others to develop skills to help them deal and cope with the numerous and nuanced challenges that they encounter. With self-love and humor at its core, it's an approachable source for helping manage one's mental health and wellness."

—**Shea Couleé,** world-renowned drag queen, actor, musician, designer, activist, and model residing in Chicago, IL

"Steff Du Bois is a one-of-a-kind personality that has created a one-of-a-kind healing tool. Yet, it's relatable to everyone! Du Bois breaks down the basics of psychology in a way that is easy to understand, and then shares practical exercises that give you a straightforward plan on how to take charge of your own healing journey. He makes therapy accessible to everyone. What a gift!"

—**Miss Angelina,** award-winning writer, director, actress, and recording artist from Puerto Rico, selected for the National Hispanic Media Coalition Latinx Showcase

"Many of us are simply not OK. Steff Du Bois's book is refreshing and practical; engagingly written, normalizing the complexity of feelings and struggles that seem part of everyday life. Each chapter is grounded in theory-driven solutions, making the book a resource for those wise enough to read it."

—**Robert Garofalo, MD, MPH,** professor of pediatrics at Northwestern University's Feinberg School of Medicine, and chief of the Division of Adolescent and Young Adult Medicine at Lurie Children's Hospital in Chicago, IL

"Steff Du Bois has done an excellent job making cognitive behavioral therapy (CBT) simple and relatable for everyday people struggling with real-life problems. Their book has something for everyone. Du Bois has created one short chapter for each week of the year, a regular bite-sized nugget of wisdom and guidance to help people feel a little more okay when they are not okay, managing an imperfect life in a flawed universe."

—**Monnica T. Williams,** board-certified clinical psychologist, professor, and Canada Research Chair in Mental Health Disparities at the University of Ottawa

"This book is for anyone eager to feel better. Written with great heart, intelligence, and wisdom, *I'm Not Okay and That's Okay* is a wonderfully accessible synthesis of our common struggles with a clear guide for what to do about them. Skills-based and grounded in CBT, it provides a road map, cleverly packaged in small, manageable steps for change that will bring relief, hope, and inspiration."

—**Karen Skerrett, PhD,** psychologist, consultant, former clinical associate professor, staff at The Family Institute at Northwestern University, and author of *Growing Married*

For my clients—past, present, and future.

Y'all inspire me every day with your courage and commitment to change.

Thank you for collaboratively generating many of the concepts and skills in this book, in our work together.

Introduction

Nobody's Always Okay, Because Struggle Is Inevitable

I wrote this book to normalize being "not okay," and to give you tools to deal with life's inevitable challenges.

With that in mind, it's time for a collective confession: We all have moments of being not okay. Why? Because each of us lives in a world of intersecting stressors and systems of oppression, and these inevitably result in feeling overwhelmed, distressed, and unable to cope. Being not okay is the emotional equivalent of experiencing physiological evolutionary cues, like thirst, hunger, or cold. It tells us we're facing one of life's inevitable struggles and that we need *something* to help us cope.

Despite the inevitability of being not okay, it remains generally stigmatized (Corrigan, Druss, and Perlick 2014). Well, not here. Here is where we accept being not okay, identify our specific struggles, and develop the skills to deal with them.

I'll Go First

Before we focus on your struggles, I'll tell you about mine. It's only fair.

Hi! My name is Steff. Nice to meet you. My pronouns are he/they.

I experience many moments of being not okay. I'm a licensed clinical psychologist who's seen hundreds of clients and given thousands of hours of therapy. I'm also an associate professor who teaches and trains students who are studying psychology. I think I'm good at my jobs, and I know how to help others grow and change. Simultaneously, I'm often not okay.

I'm queer and gender nonconforming—identities that I'm proud of, but which have led to bullying, stigma, pain, and trauma. I'm multiracial, but am white passing, so I benefit from white privilege. I'm from a single-parent, working-class home. We struggled to pay bills and make rent. I switched schools five times before seventh grade. My mom worked a lot, so growing up I'd often make my own meals, do my own homework, call the electric company because the bill was in my name—shit like that. I now have a chronic health condition that often causes pain and limits my mobility. I've received therapy multiple times throughout my life, for work-related stress, anxiety, my queerness, and challenges with intimacy.

When I'm not okay, it's probably for different reasons than when you're not okay. We've all experienced different stressors and resultant struggles. Nonetheless, we can empathize with each other in having struggled, and in our shared experience of being not okay.

This Book

Now that you know more about me, let's talk about the book.

Both the struggles and skills in this book come from my 15+ years providing therapy to clients—exploring their thoughts, feelings, behaviors; associations between these things; my clients' relationships with themselves, others, and the world around them; their past, present, and future.

I've funneled these experiences into 52 chapters. Each has a potential struggle, a skill to use, and a "How to Deal" section with an activity to promote practice and acquisition of the skill. Some chapters throughout the book discuss related struggles, but each chapter offers a unique skill.

Each chapter title either describes the unique skill or is meant to be an aphoristic entrée to the topic. I often use wordplay and acronyms, make puns, and share anecdotes as an on-ramp to chapters. This isn't to belittle being not okay. Instead, it's to honor my clients' feedback over the years that it's important to balance discussion of being not okay with lighter content, memorable context, and sometimes unrelated framing devices.

The book also lays out my own theory of change and its key components, in the first ten-ish chapters. These chapters are the foundation upon which the rest of the book is built. I recommend everyone work through these first—even if you know your specific struggles already.

After you've established this foundation, you can do the subsequent chapters in order, or you can pick and choose. As you tackle the individual struggles in subsequent chapters and learn more skills, you could consider revisiting the early chapters again. You could complete one chapter weekly—this would fit with a year of weekly therapy in which each session focuses on a different topic/skill. Or make your way through the book at whatever pace works for you.

As you work through the book, you may want to take notes—in the book or in an adjunctive journal or notebook—recording your reflections, notes, and completed activities from each chapter.

The Skills Are CBT-Based

By "CBT-based," I mean their origins are in cognitive behavior therapy (Beck and Beck 2011). CBT is generally effective for lots of common struggles (Tolin 2016), which makes it a useful source for the skills here.

CBT understands each person through the following framework, simplified and modified a bit by me:

Past Experiences → Core Beliefs → Current Situation → Automatic Thought

→ **Explanation for Automatic Thought** → **Emotions** → **Behaviors** → **Physiology**

CBT says our *past experiences* may produce deep-seated *core beliefs* about ourselves or the world. When we're in various *situations* later in life, our established *core beliefs* can influence the *automatic thoughts* we have, the *explanation* we generate for having automatic thoughts, and our subsequent *emotions, behaviors,* and *physiology*.

CBT rightly asserts that it's frequently hard to change the situations we're in. But we can change our thoughts about and in these situations—so they're more effective and accurate. These new thoughts can then positively influence our emotions, behaviors, and physiology—thus enhancing our experience of each situation, and of life more broadly.

Let's say your past experiences include your siblings relentlessly teasing you while growing up. You could've formed the core belief *Something's wrong with me*. Nowadays, when you're in stressful situations, a related, automatic thought might pop up—something like *I must've done something wrong*. You might erroneously explain having this automatic thought by concluding *It's true*. The emotions of *guilt, regret,* and *self-doubt* may follow. You may *apologize, become quiet,* or *leave the situation*. You may start *sweating* or *feeling dizzy*.

CBT dissects this situation, focusing on correcting your automatic thought so it matches reality instead of matching your past core belief.

Ready to Be Not Okay Together?

Whenever you're ready, turn this page of this book, right into the next chapter of your life—a chapter with more effective thinking, less emotional overwhelm, healthier behaviors, improved relationships, and more self-love.

By the end of the book, you'll still experience moments of being not okay. But you'll have tools to deal with those moments.

1

Check, Please!

Struggle: understanding what's wrong

It's super common to know *that* you're not okay, but to not understand *why*. Like those days you wake up feeling off but can't explain where the off feeling is coming from. Or the days when you're short-tempered but can't think of a reason. This can be confusing and disempowering, and it can amplify your experience of being not okay. That's why it's important to identify what's making you not okay and to create related goals that address the problem.

Identifying why you're not okay gives a name and shape to your otherwise amorphous experience (Beck and Beck 2011). To assess why you're not okay, you can use something I call a "check-in checklist"—when you check in on yourself with a checklist of items relevant to your well-being. Another term you'll see for such check-ins is "self-monitoring" (Tolin 2016).

Your checklist items could be the things CBT says to pay attention to: the situation you're in, your thoughts, emotions, behaviors, and physiology (Beck and Beck 2011). Or you could design a more you-specific checklist based on what you know about yourself, e.g., sleep, sadness, exercise, work stress, diet, etc.

Whatever items are on your check-in checklist, run down the list one by one, assessing where you're at on each item. For example: What situation are you in currently? What thoughts are you having? What kind of sleep did you get recently? What's going on at work? Etc.

Sometimes doing a check-in checklist yields some pretty upsetting and overwhelming results. Like when you take your car in for an oil change and the mechanic tells you there are five other repairs that need addressing.

On the flip side, doing a check-in checklist provides important insight into why you're currently not okay. Plus, once you identify current challenges, stressors, or struggles, you can use that information to create associated goals to work toward.

To create such goals, take whatever was problematic from your check-in checklist, and flip it so it reads as a positive goal that'll make you feel better.

For example, if during my check-in checklist I conclude I'm having self-critical thoughts, I can create the related goal *praising myself more*. If my check-in checklist indicates I'm feeling socially anxious, I can make the goal *feeling less anxious around others*. If I realize from the checklist that I'm unable to focus because I'm hungover, I can generate the goal *drinking less alcohol*.

Some people prefer to get concrete here—making goals like *praising myself five times each day* or *drinking ten drinks weekly, max*. You also can use rating scales when you make goals, e.g., *rating my mood 7 or above on a scale of 1 to 10—with 10 being high—at least four days per week*. More on these scales soon.

This exercise will be useful as you read this book, and more broadly as you strive to live life in a self-aware and happy way.

How to Deal

1. Create a list of five-ish items for your personal check-in checklist. These items can be anything that's made you feel not okay in the past.
2. Make the list in a place that's easy to find—on your phone, in an email to yourself, or on a sticky note you keep in your backpack.
3. Run through the list either when you're feeling not okay, on a fixed schedule like once weekly, or both.
4. For each item, list recent/current details of your experience.
5. For anything that's making you feel not okay, flip it to create a related goal that, when achieved, could help you feel better.

2

Connect the Dots

Struggle: *recognizing what relates to what*

A central tenet of CBT is that there's a reciprocal association between the multiple components of our experience: the situation we're in, and our thoughts, emotions, behaviors, and physiology during that situation (Tolin 2016). These factors all interact and influence each other, positively or negatively. Recognizing how these factors relate to each other, aka connecting the dots between them, is a foundational skill we can use when we're not okay.

Using this skill yields two payoffs. First, it extends the insight you cultivated in chapter 1 with your check-in checklist, thereby facilitating a deeper understanding of yourself that may make situations less overwhelming. Second, it provides you with potential points of intervention when trying to change your experience.

Let's say you're at the doctor's office, awaiting results of a serious medical test. You're understandably feeling not okay. Let's say that next, to understand what's wrong, you do your check-in checklist from chapter 1—assessing the things CBT suggests: current thoughts, emotions, behaviors, and physiology. You realize your mind is racing with various thoughts, e.g., *I'm going to die*. You're feeling multiple emotions, but namely *fear*. For behaviors, you're *tapping your foot rapidly*. Physiologically, your *heart is racing*.

It's good to know all this information about your experience. But if you want to change something about it, you'll likely need to understand how these facets of your experience relate to each other. For example, the thought *I'm going to die* may make you feel *fearful*. Extending this, the feeling of *fear* may *increase your heart rate*, which may relate to you *tapping your foot rapidly*.

After connecting the dots between these pieces of your experience, you can assess which piece is most easy to intervene on. CBT says that's usually the *thought* (Beck and Beck 2011; Tolin 2016). This is because we usually can't just change a situation, make ourselves feel an emotion, or alter our physiology. But we may be able to change what we're thinking.

And because thoughts relate to the other pieces of our experience, if we can change our thought, then our emotions, behaviors, and physiology may follow.

Going back to our example, if we can change the thought *I'm going to die* to something less negative, like *I'm going to be okay* or even *I won't get the worst news*, then we may feel more *hopeful*—or at least less *fearful*. Our *heart rate also may decrease*, and our *foot tapping may recede* because we're less nervous.

We'll talk more soon about how to change your thoughts. But for now, let's practice the skill of recognizing associations between the multiple components of moments when you're not okay, focusing on your thoughts specifically. This will set you up for success down the road when you actively try changing your thoughts.

How to Deal

1. You can piggyback off the check-in checklist activity to complete this one. If your list doesn't include *thoughts* and *emotions* from the CBT list, add these—to practice the skill of connecting thoughts to emotions and other things.
2. After you've completed a check-in checklist that includes thoughts and emotions, ask yourself how the components on your checklist may relate to each other.
3. Draw this out, making circles to write your thoughts, emotions, etc. in, and then using arrows to draw links between these. This helps you literally see the connections between the multiple components of your current experience.
4. Keep copies of each one of these you draw out. After you've accumulated a handful, review them all together. Look for patterns or themes, writing them out using the

format "When I think _____, I feel _____." For example, "When I think self-critical thoughts, I feel worthless or sad." You'll use this information and insight throughout the book.

3

Pooh-Pooh Because It's True

Struggle: *believing your automatic thoughts*

Many thoughts on your check-in checklists will be *automatic thoughts*. These thoughts pop up uninvitedly, are ubiquitous, and are frequently negative. For this reason, multiple chapters in this book (e.g., 3, 6, 8, 11, 14) provide skills to respond to various automatic thoughts.

Examples of automatic thoughts include: *I'm incompetent* while you're working, *They're judging me* when talking to someone, *I need a drink* when you've committed to abstaining from alcohol, *I'll be single forever* when you're relaxing at home alone, and *I'm going to fail* when you're about to take a test.

Automatic thoughts strongly influence our experience of whatever moment we're in. They can both fill our head with negative narration and negatively influence our subsequent emotions, behaviors, and physiological reactions (Beck and Beck, 2011; Tolin 2016).

Yet, we can intervene on automatic thoughts—thus reducing their negative impact on us. The front-line intervention strategy is to explain to ourselves why we had the automatic thought in the first place.

I'd say most of the time, we assume we have a thought *because it's true*. We don't question the thought, and in fact within milliseconds, we accept it as accurate. In fact, *I had that thought because it's true* can itself be considered a secondary, or semi-, automatic thought (Tolin 2016).

In truth, there's no reason to assume we have an automatic thought *because it's true*. Some of us may have 1,000 automatic thoughts per day; could those all be objective, accurate, factual statements? No way! And in fact, that sounds like a boring 1,000 thoughts to have. Thus, we can dismiss, reject, or *pooh-pooh* the explanation *because it's true*.

Once we pooh-pooh *because it's true*, we can generate alternative explanations for having the automatic thought. Eventually, we can land on a new explanation for the automatic thought—one that's things like compassionate, forgiving, or even positive

Let's use the example from above, *I need a drink*. Why might you have this automatic thought—other than just *because it's true*?

Well, maybe because your body is used to having a drink at this time of night. Or because you're stressed and want to relax. Maybe you're thirsty and need water. Maybe you just heard the clink of someone else's glass, and your brain associates that clink with a drink. Maybe your mom used to say the phrase each night after work. Etc.

After generating multiple alternative explanations for having an automatic thought, you can usually see that your default explanation, *because it's true*, is likely not the most valid explanation.

The implication here is that a significant proportion of your automatic thoughts aren't worth believing. Like Ron Burgundy, that's kind of a big deal.

Using the skill pooh-pooh *because it's true* repeatedly will teach you that automatic thoughts are powerless. They only have power when we give them power—by believing them at face value.

How to Deal

1. Complete a check-in checklist now, assessing your negative automatic thoughts specifically. Or, list some negative automatic thoughts you know you have frequently.
2. Pick one of these thoughts to fill in the following blank: "I had the automatic thought _____, *because it's true*."
3. Connect the dots between this statement and an emotion: How does this statement make you feel?

4. Pooh-pooh *because it's true*, by generating an alternative explanation for it. Repeat the statement in #2 using this alternative explanation.
5. Connect the dots between this new statement and an emotion: How does this new statement makes you feel?
6. Repeat #4 and #5 until you generate and believe an alternative explanation that makes you feel better than *because it's true*.

4

Tiny Interventions

Struggle: *how to change, part 1*

The pooh-pooh *because it's true* skill is an example of an "intervention"—a word I define as "any purposeful attempt to change something." In the last chapter, that "something" was your explanation for having an automatic thought.

More broadly, I reference interventions a fair amount in this book because they're a primary tool you can use to make meaningful changes in your life (Tolin 2016).

The effectiveness of interventions is often tested using expensive, long-term research studies that include hundreds or even thousands of participants. But you don't need this "big" approach to trying interventions and seeing if they're effective.

Instead, you can practice tiny interventions, in which you alter one small thing about yourself or your environment, and then assess if it helps you change.

Most interventions you'll be asked to try in this book will be "tiny" in nature. You'll likely try changing something minuscule to reach a related goal. For example, you could change the time you wake up to try reaching the goal of being more productive. You could change what you eat for breakfast to try reaching the goal of having more energy in the morning. You could change where you keep something to try reaching the goal of using that something more, or less. Stuff like that.

The phrase "tiny interventions" also includes diminutive language. This is a purposeful linguistic choice, meant to convey the nature of the work that actually produces change—tiny things you practice until they stick or start a positive cascade of change.

You've probably heard related cliché phrases, things like "Change takes time" and "Step by step." This is a time when the clichés are true. Sure, sometimes we can change rapidly. But most often, tiny interventions are a necessary first step in the larger, stepwise change process.

It's important not just to do tiny interventions, but also to assess their effectiveness. You can make this assessment qualitatively—asking yourself questions about the current *quality* of things. Like, "How did that go?" and "Did that help?" Or you can write a few sentences about how you're doing or how a tiny intervention is working. This is definitely good data to collect on your experience.

You also can collect quantitative data—when you use specific numbers or labels to rate your experience. For example, you can rate your mood using a 1 (low) to 10 (high) scale. Or use 1 to 100 if you want more nuance. You also could rate your mood using labels like "low, medium, high" or "worse, same, better" compared to sometime before.

Quantitative data is useful because it gives you concrete evidence whether the tiny intervention is making things better. Plus, it's self-reinforcing to see your numbers or labels change in a positive direction.

Trying tiny interventions, plus collecting some data on your experience, will facilitate deeper insight and change.

How to Deal

1. Use your work in previous chapters to select a "target" for your tiny intervention. Targets are the things that, after doing a check-in checklist, you conclude are feeling off—and that you want to change.
2. Using a suggested scale above, give yourself a quantitative rating of where you're currently at with this thing.
3. Ask questions about the what, when, and where of this target: What's happening with my thoughts, feelings, behaviors? When does it occur, and what precedes it? Where does it occur?
4. Select one thing to intervene on related to the target—something related to the what, when, or where of it.

5. Specify your tiny intervention. What is the change you're going to make?
6. Make this change once, and then assess how it went by giving yourself a new quantitative rating of how off you feel now—using the same scale you did earlier.
7. If you want, also use qualitative data to assess the effectiveness of your tiny intervention.

5

TEAPOT on Repeat

Struggle: *how to change, part 2*

While tiny interventions can get you started on the road to change, TEAPOT on repeat is the nuts and bolts of your change process.

There's basically a well-established formula for change. And it's not, as they say, rocket science—it's much simpler. This formula provides the first of several acronyms we'll use as we build skills: TEAPOT.

TEAPOT stands for "trial, error, and practice over time."

Trial, error is a process of trying a new strategy, inevitably making mistakes while trying the new strategy, assessing what you learned from the error, and using what you learned to try another new strategy—over and over again (*practice over time;* Wolpe 1990), until you find a strategy that works.

When you're not okay, for whatever reason, you can use the skills from chapters 1 and 2 to get insight into what's going on. You then can use the skills from chapters 3 and 4 to make small but meaningful changes. And then, when you want to dig in—creating a continuous feedback loop of *intervene, collect data, use that data to inform next steps*—TEAPOT on repeat is your skill.

Let's use an example I've experienced personally, and one I hear about commonly in my work with clients: Each year, during the shortened days of the winter months, we can feel sad.

You can use your check-in checklist to assess what thoughts and emotions you're having during these times. For thoughts, perhaps *Everything sucks, Here we go again,* or *I hate this time of year*. For emotions, certainly *sad*, but also maybe *unmotivated* or *hopeless*. We'd hypothesize here that your negative thoughts connect to your negative emotions.

Perhaps, as a tiny intervention on your negative thoughts, you place pictures of your favorite memories around your apartment—one in each dresser drawer, one inside each kitchen cabinet, one on each door, etc. The hope is that seeing these images regularly will remind you of happy times, generate some positive thoughts about those times, and decrease your sadness.

Placing the pictures in your apartment is not just a tiny intervention—it's also your first *trial*. If seeing the happy pictures for one or two weeks makes you feel less sad and more motivated, keep the picture intervention going!

If this first *trial* doesn't work, you can assess why. Perhaps the pictures include friends you no longer speak to, which makes you more sad, not less sad. Learning from this *error* in your *trial*, you can try a new approach: maybe printing pictures with current friends and replacing the old pictures with these new ones. You'd then *practice over time* this different, new strategy.

TEAPOT, on repeat.

TEAPOT on repeat can be used when you want to change your thoughts, behaviors, relationships with others, and more. It's a key skill that'll help you feel more aware of your experience, in control of your experience, and able to change the parts of your experience that cause distress.

How to Deal

1. Identify a target you want to change. You can either use something from an earlier "How to Deal" exercise, or pick a different unpleasant thought, emotion, or behavior.
2. Create a first *trial* by trying a tiny intervention related to your target.
3. Practice this tiny intervention over time, collecting quantitative or qualitative data for one or two weeks.
4. After one or two weeks, use your collected data to assess how successful the *trial* has been, what *errors* occurred, and what you've learned.

5. If the *trial* hasn't been totally successful, use what you've learned to create a new, improved *trial*.
6. *Practice* this new trial *over time*—once again collecting data, and once again for one or two weeks.
7. Repeat, until the thought, emotion, behavior, etc. improves.

6

Scooby-You

Struggle: *inaccurate or anxious thoughts*

Scooby-Doo, Where Are You!—a childhood staple for many of us. It was a show that balanced vintage fun fashion, a light cartoon vibe, and tales of crime and betrayal.

Scooby and the gang taught us some valuable life lessons. First, be a detective: Find clues to help solve your mystery. Second, the villain's often there all along—someone secretly sabotaging an otherwise groovy situation.

We can turn these lessons into skills and apply them when we struggle with inaccurate or anxious thoughts. Such thoughts are often automatic thoughts, although not always—like when you're ruminating about whether you forgot your keys at home, even though you hear them jingling in your pocket. Inaccurate or anxious thoughts can be extreme or subtle, critical or nagging, mean or sad. In any case, they make us feel not okay—despite the fact they don't reflect reality!

When these thoughts pop up, be a detective—not Scooby-Doo, but Scooby-You.

Let's use another example I've experienced personally and one I hear about commonly with my clients. Every time your romantic partner's phone rings, buzzes, or vibrates, you have a negative reaction. Let's dig deeper to find that when their phone goes off, you think something like, *They're cheating on me.* This relates to feeling *anger* or *distrust*, and to having *tense conversations with your partner.*

Let's play detective with this thought. Like a detective, ask yourself, *What's the evidence for, and against, my thought that my partner is cheating on me?* (Beck and Beck 2011). To collect evidence, you can recall past experiences with your partner, asking related questions such as, *Has my partner lied to me before? Have they cheated on me? Do they have a history of cheating? Have they done anything remotely sketchy at all?* Ask as many related questions as you want, answering each with facts, not hunches or feelings.

Playing detective like this often helps establish that there isn't sufficient evidence for a thought to be true—thus exposing the villain of the situation to be your own inaccurate thoughts. Instead of sending this villain to jail, you can try to correct the inaccurate thought to one that actually fits the evidence. In our example, it might be *I have the automatic thought that they're cheating on me, but there's no evidence to back it up.*

Sometimes being Scooby-You and playing detective leads you to conclude the original thought was accurate. When this happens, admittedly, it can hit you hard. But even then, at least what's hitting you hard is reality, not an erroneous interpretation of reality.

More commonly, playing detective with inaccurate or anxious thoughts—and exposing those thoughts for what they are—will direct your attention, emotion, and time to thoughts that are true. This will ground your cognitive experience in reality—which in most cases means your emotions, behavior, and physiology will fluctuate less, and you'll enjoy life more.

How to Deal

1. Using a check-in checklist, or your own insight and past experiences, identify an unpleasant or anxious thought that you have repeatedly. Write it down—often this, in itself, helps people see its inaccuracy.
2. Be Scooby-You, by examining the evidence for and against this thought. Consider writing this down also, as seeing the evidence on both sides might help you evaluate whether the thought is accurate.
3. If you conclude the thought is inaccurate, ask, *What's an alternative thought I could have—one that is more evidence-based?* Generate this thought, basing it on the evidence you collected.
4. Practice this thought by saying it or writing it down repeatedly.

5. If you conclude the thought is accurate, first give yourself sympathy. Then, decide if you're going to take any action based on the thought being true.

7

Time to Flex

Struggle: *knowing your strengths or current tools*

My students and younger clients have taught me that to "flex" means to show what you're capable of, or even to show off a bit.

Well, I think it's time for you to flex. Specifically, to take inventory of your current strengths or tools that help you cope when you're not okay.

We've already discussed some new tools: the check-in checklist, connecting the dots, pooh-pooh *because it's true*, TEAPOT on repeat, playing detective as Scooby-You. But the truth is, you probably started reading this book with at least a few unique strengths of your own. Knowing what those are, and using them at the right time, will help you move forward in this book and in life.

A common response to the above is something like, "I don't have any strengths," or "I have strengths, but they won't help me feel better when I'm struggling."

First, those sound like quintessential automatic or inaccurate thoughts that you can use pooh-pooh *because it's true* or Scooby-You with. ☺ Second, I totally hear you, and I've had the same thoughts about myself.

But hear me out: We're all good at *something*, and that something may help us when we're floundering.

Let's use the basic CBT categories of situations, thoughts, emotions, and behaviors to brainstorm your strengths and coping skills. For situations, strengths may include resources we have or positive situations we find ourselves in: regular therapy, a community of loved ones, access to a relaxing park nearby. For thoughts, strengths include thinking clearly under pressure, thinking positively in times of stress, or not assuming the worst is happening. For emotions, strengths include staying calm under duress, not being quick to anger, and being patient. For behaviors, strengths include taking deep breaths to relax, sleeping consistently, sticking to a schedule, and moderating substance use.

There are plenty of other potential strengths and tools that aren't listed above, e.g., creative expression, attention to detail, emotional awareness, holding yourself accountable, making friends easily, learning new skills quickly, etc.

These strengths and tools can be leveraged to help you cope during stressful life moments and to help you change the problematic cognitive, emotional, and behavioral patterns you'll identify throughout this book.

Taking stock of what you do well also helps you realize what's currently not one of your strengths. Developing new strengths and tools can become one of your goals, if you'd like. The more you have, the more likely you are to deal with your struggles efficiently and effectively.

How to Deal

1. List as many personal strengths and tools you can think of. Use the above CBT categories to organize your list, but also feel free to go outside these categories.
2. If you can, ask some friends or loved ones what they think your strengths are. Often others see strengths in us that we don't.
3. Reflect on a few past and current struggles that you've successfully dealt with. Write out a few sentences describing how you successfully dealt with each struggle. What strengths or tools did you use?
4. Review these, adding any emergent strengths or tools to the list you started above.
5. Consult this list moving forward. You can use whatever's on it to effect change.

8

Miss Interpretation

Struggle: *seeing things negatively*

Fun fact: On my phone, I have a running list of drag queen names that I've made up. My favorite is DeNise DeNephew, but another name on the list is inspired by CBT: Miss Interpretation.

One theme of CBT is that our personal interpretation of any moment very strongly influences our experience of that moment (Beck and Beck 2011). By "interpretation," I mean a thought or assumption we have that's supposed to make sense of the moment.

Something happens around us; then, we interpret that something with a thought. More than the something itself, our interpretation of the something influences how we feel about it. On and on, every day.

This strongly relates to chapter 3: Just like we can generate false explanations for why we're having negative automatic thoughts, we can generate false interpretations for what's happening around us.

Problem is, these inaccurate, negative *misinterpretations* of the people and things around us cause much unwarranted stress, sadness, and anger.

The classic example is when you walk by someone, smile at them, and they scowl back at you.

How would you interpret this scowl? Take a moment to generate a few different thoughts or assumptions you'd have in response to the scowl.

Many people might interpret the scowl by assuming something negative: *They don't like me*, or *Is there something stuck in my teeth?*, or *That person's a real (expletive)*. And the truth is, the person may not like you, something may be stuck in your teeth, and they may be a (expletive).

But it's perhaps equally likely that a more neutral, or even positive, interpretation of the scowl is accurate. Something like *They may be in pain*, *They could've gotten some bad news*, or as a positive interpretation, *They're not scowling; they're making a funny face to make me laugh*.

Our interpretations are important because they drive other parts of our experience—namely, our emotions. Generally, negative interpretations lead to negative emotions, positive interpretations to positive emotions, and neutral interpretations to neutral emotions.

With this in mind, try to catch yourself making negative interpretations of what others say or do. And then, try to generate an alternative interpretation that's more positive or neutral. Use TEAPOT on repeat to practice different iterations of this and assess if over time you're generally feeling more positive.

But what if your negative interpretation is accurate? This is a legit question, just like, What if playing detective leads to concluding the original thought was accurate?

Absolutely, sometimes you want to act after making a negative interpretation. In our example, you might say to the person who scowled, "Hey, I think you scowled. Is everything okay?" I suggest making a rule for yourself—something like, *I'll only react to negative interpretations if something really bothers me. Otherwise, I won't breathe life into the situation.*

But even if your negative interpretation is accurate, you can ask yourself, *Is it effective to interpret things that way?* Negative interpretations make you feel bad, and often there's nothing you can do about others scowling at you. So, try resisting the urge to linger in negative interpretations. You can guide yourself away from negative interpretations with a thought that's more descriptive, e.g., *They scowled at me. Now I'm just gonna keep going about my day.*

Incorporating more positive and neutral interpretations of situations will make you less stressed and less reactive to things that don't deserve your attention anyway.

How to Deal

1. Each day for one week, use check-in checklists to identify a moment when you felt bad.
2. Connect the dots between the *situation*, *thought*, and *emotion* for each moment, with *thought* here being represented by your interpretation. Describe the *situation* in one sentence, note how you interpreted it with another sentence, and then report how you *felt*.
3. Generate an alternative interpretation to the situation—one that's more positive or neutral, even if you don't believe it.
4. Note how this new interpretation could make you *feel* and compare it to the original *emotion* you had in the *situation*.
5. TEAPOT on repeat to acquire this skill over the long term.

9
Do Self-Compassion

Struggle: *self-critique*

Self-compassion is to mental health what water is to physical health. It's basically something we need every day to survive and be healthy. And if we don't get it for an extended period of time, we can start to deteriorate.

But like, what is it?

I define "self-compassion" as "giving yourself sympathy, kindness, and love, especially in times of suffering and self-critique" (Neff 2003). If you're like most people, you give others compassion more easily than you give it to yourself.

That's one reason it's important for us to *do* self-compassion—to allocate time, energy, thoughts, and behaviors to practice giving ourselves compassion. The more we do it, the better we'll get at it.

Another reason to do self-compassion is that we may not get compassion from others. Being able to trust yourself as a constant source of self-compassion is like a superpower that will help you manage and overcome your struggles.

Importantly, *doing* self-compassion builds a bridge to *feeling* self-compassion. The feeling of self-compassion is like any artistic endeavor: It doesn't exist until we create it. Until then, it's conceptual and less impactful than when it's tangible.

Finally, and related to the last point, doing self-compassion keeps us accountable for supporting ourselves. It's one thing to say we're self-compassionate; it's another to do self-compassionate things.

Self-compassion is related to self-care (see chapter 19), insofar as both suggest a positive self-focus. They're different, in that self-care aims to increase well-being broadly, while self-compassion aims to cultivate positive self-directed *emotions* specifically.

But like, how do you do it?

You can define what self-compassion looks like for you. Scan recent and distant memories to recollect things you *did* that made you feel more kind and forgiving, and less critical and guilty.

Beyond this, I work with clients to cultivate a few specific skills.

First, make a list of self-compassionate thoughts in your own words. Review it once every week/month, and also when acute self-critique pops up.

Second, when you're feeling self-critical about something, generate sympathetic, contextual explanations for what happened. If you're angry with yourself for being late to an important meeting, you might say, *I was late for multiple reasons that were out of my control. I needed to eat first, and traffic was bad. Plus, I was stressed, and the stress probably scrambled my brain.*

Third, and this may sound strange to some people: Literally hug yourself, while saying loving things to yourself. This type of moment is often what we haven't gotten enough of from others in our life—which is the very reason self-compassion may be tough to feel now. So, give yourself these moments now.

Finally, things like performing acts of kindness toward yourself, connecting with others on the fact that nobody's perfect, and tuning in to the present moment instead of self-critical thoughts can facilitate self-compassion (Neff 2003).

You'll see the term "self-compassion" a lot in this book. Now, you have a roadmap for how to feel self-compassion: *Do* it.

How to Deal

1. Rate yourself on your current level of self-compassion, using something like 1 (low) to 10 (high).
2. List five to ten things you could *do* to feel kind, loving, and sympathetic toward yourself. Schedule one or two of these into your day, for two weeks.
3. After you complete this, rerate yourself on self-compassion.

4. Pick other items from the list you made in #2, either one by one or in combination, and practice them over time.
5. Rerate yourself on self-compassion every couple months to see if doing self-compassion is making you feel more self-compassionate.
6. Add to this list over time, as you learn more about how you can facilitate feeling self-compassion.

10

The Dud at Your Party

Struggle: *things you can't change*

While CBT is mostly change-focused, it recognizes that some things aren't changeable—either at all, or in the current moment. Even with our best change strategies, things like anxious thoughts, physical pain, or guilt inevitably hit us hard and stick around.

Each of these is like the dud at your otherwise fun party.

Just imagine your party. Cute decorations, good music, tasty food, refreshing drinks, and cool guests talking about even cooler things.

But alas, there's one person there who's basically the worst. They're totally killing the vibe: turning down the music, complaining about the food and drinks, interrupting good conversation to tell off-kilter jokes.

What if we can't just kick out this dud? What if they linger the whole night? In these times—with our literal parties and with our mental health struggles that aren't responsive to change strategies—we can use strategies from acceptance and commitment therapy (ACT; Hayes et al. 2011).

ACT (said like the first *act* of a play) is a branch of CBT that asserts we don't need to *change* the negative parts of our lives. Instead, we can accept these things are present, change our relationship to these things so they affect us less, and commit to living a meaningful and happy life despite their existence (Hayes et al. 2011). I like to say these strategies help us "calmly coexist" with our struggles instead of wrestling with and trying to defeat them.

Some specific ACT strategies are discussed elsewhere in the book (chapters 21, 32, 46). Here, as a broader introduction to ACT, let's discuss some foundational strategies: acceptance, attunement, and defusion (Hayes et al. 2011).

Acceptance strategies include positive self-talk, such as *Thank you, thought,* and *I welcome this negative emotion and will live my life with it.* The key here is to *actually* welcome the thought or emotion, not just say you welcome them—something that can be accomplished by, e.g., framing each thought as an ineffective but benevolent attempt to cope with the current situation.

"Attunement" means deeper connection with the moment or with some part of the moment that is pleasant or neutral. Attunement is a combination of relaxing into the moment and having laser-like focus in the moment. Attunement can reduce the impact of, e.g., negative thoughts on you, because attuning to your current moment shifts attention away from the negative thoughts angling for your attention. The negative thoughts are still there, but you relate to them less strongly.

Defusion is when you create distance between the negative thing and the rest of your experience. Defusion strategies include saying or thinking, *I'm having the thought* _____, to remind yourself that you are separate from your thoughts. If you'd like to add to this, include sensory statements that also promote attunement. For example, *I'm having the thought* _____ *while I smell a mahogany candle, hear the hum of my radiator, and feel my dog lying on my feet.*

Broadly, ACT strategies promote effectively allocating your resources: your attention, time, energy, thoughts, emotions, and physical self. If you can effectively allocate these, you can change your relationship to bothersome thoughts, emotions, and physical experiences, and learn to live with just about any dud trying to ruin your party.

How to Deal

1. Identify a current dud at your party—a stressor you can't just change or get rid of.
2. Rate how bothersome you find this dud currently, using either a numerical scale or a "low, medium, high" rating.

3. Pick one type of ACT strategy to use on this dud: acceptance, attunement, defusion. Or, even visualizing the "dud" metaphor is ACT-based and can be used.
4. Use these strategies on the dud for one week. Rerate how bothersome you find the dud.
5. Keep experimenting and collecting data, by using different ACT strategies on this and other duds you can't change or get rid of.

11

C You Later!

Struggle: *negative thoughts*

The content of our thoughts strongly determines how we experience life. For example, if you look in the mirror and have the negative thought *Nobody likes me,* then that becomes the narrative that dictates your self-perception. If you can flip the content of such negative thoughts—making them more positive—your self-perception will be more positive, and you'll be happier.

If controlling our negative thought content is the goal, we can use the "four Cs" to get there. The first three Cs are a common CBT strategy (Tolin 2016); I've added the fourth when working with clients.

First, **catch** the negative thought. To catch a thought is to become *nonjudgmentally aware* of it, without buying into its content. You might say, *There's that thought.*

Second, **check** how accurate the thought is. You can use your Scooby-You skills here, e.g., asking, *Is that a fact? What's the evidence for or against it?*

Next, for thoughts you catch, check, and determine are untrue, try to **change** them. This is most commonly done by flipping the content of the thought to its opposite, or by generating a new thought based on the evidence you just collected.

Lastly, do the above with **compassion**, specifically by trying to understand where this negative thought may have originated. It's never your fault when a negative thought pops into your head. In fact, the thought probably came from another person or time in your life—a parent, bully, etc. You deserve sympathy for having the thought now.

Let's use the four Cs now to respond to the thought *Nobody likes me*.

First, catch the thought without criticizing yourself for having it. You could say, *The thought 'Nobody likes me' just popped up*.

Next, check, *Does literally no one like me?* The answer is almost definitely no.

So, let's change the thought—maybe into something more neutral like *Not everyone likes me, but some people definitely do*.

Finally, use the skill pooh-pooh *because it's true* to speculate why this thought's popping up now. Maybe you just ate your lunch alone, which triggered sad memories of eating lunch alone in high school. For eating lunch alone then and now, you deserve compassion.

How to Deal

1. Use insight, past experiences, and completed check-in checklists to catch some of your common negative thoughts. Continue adding to this list over time.
2. For each thought on your list, write out check, change, and compassion responses.
3. Repeat the new thought from each change step, by saying or writing it multiple times. This will help embed the new thought and replace the old one.
4. Eventually, after practicing the above, you'll get better at catching negative thoughts *in the moment*. For now, keep that running list of common negative thoughts from #1.

12

FOMO's Cousin DODI

Struggle: *dread, avoidance*

FOMO, or fear of missing out, is that anxious, longing feeling you get when you think others are having fun without you (Przybylski et al. 2013). I've both experienced FOMO and have had multiple clients discuss their FOMO.

In these FOMO discussions, I've generated my own related acronym to capture the opposite, yet similarly universal, experience: DODI—dread of doing it.

DODI is the feeling of anxious apprehension that creeps up as you're about to do something. It's often preceded by racing, negative thoughts, e.g., *Ugh, I don't want to do this,* or *This is gonna suck.* And it's often followed by behaviors like avoidance, procrastination, or canceling plans.

DODI isn't bad per se. At its core, it's an emotional cue that's communicating something: *I'm feeling uncomfortable now, about doing something in the future.*

What makes DODI "bad" is when we give into it unquestioningly, using it as a license to avoid things without good reason.

It's tough because when DODI leads to avoidance, we often feel relief from our discomfort. But this relief is temporary and ultimately makes it harder to do what we avoided. Stress, guilt, shame, and procrastination may follow.

Overcoming DODI can make you feel the opposite: carefree, proud, empowered, and accomplished. Plus, broadly you free up time and mental space that was occupied by your dread.

Here's how I recommend responding to DODI:

First, identify the negative, anxious thoughts that precede your DODI. Then, be Scooby-You with those thoughts, searching for evidence for or against each. If you think, *This work will take forever*, you can search for evidence for how long it will actually take. Usually you'll find counter-evidence to the DODI-related thought and can use that counter-evidence to generate a new, more accurate thought, such as *The work will probably take two hours, tops*. This new thought likely will make the task more approachable.

Next, make a contract with yourself (Tolin 2016). Something like, *I'll do the work I'm dreading for five minutes, and if I still want to stop, I will.* This approach gives your behaviors a chance to supersede your negative thoughts and DODI. You also can add healthy incentives to your contract, like *If I do the work I'm dreading, I'll take a reward nap after.*

Visualizing yourself doing the dreaded thing step-by-step also could make it more approachable (Barlow 2021; Rennie, Harris, and Webb 2014). Using the example of dreading work, you can picture yourself opening your computer, logging in to your email, opening the document you need to work on, typing the first few words, etc.

Finally, you could practice radical optimism, generating the best-case scenario of the situation. What if you do the work you're dreading, it goes quickly, and you get a promotion for doing it so well? DODI often assumes that our future experience will be the worst. Even just considering the opposite outcome could be an effective tiny intervention.

Avoid life less and live life more by using these strategies to combat DODI.

How to Deal

1. Make a list of recent times you've canceled plans, procrastinated, or just avoided something altogether.
2. For each item on the list, assess whether DODI was the culprit. (It's not DODI if, e.g., you were ill, solving an acute crisis, or didn't have the resources to do something.)
3. For the recent times that were DODI, apply the strategies above—just in your head for now.
4. The next time you feel DODI creeping in, nonjudgmentally label it "DODI."

5. Then, try the strategies above in real time, using ratings to assess which ones help decrease your avoidance and move you closer to doing the thing you dread.

13

Rewind, Be Kind

Struggle: *beating yourself up over the past*

I have a special place in my heart for VHS tapes because I worked in multiple video stores growing up. Consequently, the phrase "Be kind, rewind" became etched into my head. This phrase was how video stores implored patrons to rewind their movies before returning them—to save time on the back end for employees like me.

If we flip the order of the phrase, we get a useful skill for when we're beating ourselves up over something in our past: Rewind, be kind. This phrase suggests we look back on early life events and interpret them with kindness instead of self-blame.

Specifically, *rewind* encourages us to reflect on past life events that meet two conditions: They affected us negatively, and we blame ourselves for them. These can be big life events, like when our parents got divorced, we lost our job, or we experienced persistent bullying. Or they can be not so big, like when our parents got into a fight once, we got some feedback at work, or someone ridiculed our clothes.

Be kind encourages us to reinterpret what happened in our past—to see these events through the lens of sympathy, self-compassion, and nonjudgment. *Be kind* reminds us that whatever we've experienced in our past, there's a clear, consistent, and specific way we can look back on it: with kindness to ourselves.

Each of us can look back on a past moment and think, *I did something wrong, That was my fault,* or *I'm a bad person.* Instead of believing these thoughts, we can generate generous and sympathetic interpretations of past moments, e.g., *What happened was not my fault.*

And indeed, it very likely wasn't your fault. Your past self didn't ask to make a mistake, to be imperfect, or to fail at something. And your current self, well, they don't deserve to suffer for what happened in the past. You can help your present self suffer less, by looking back at past "mistakes" and reinterpreting them more kindly.

RIP, VHS. With your demise, we can no longer "Be kind, rewind." However, as we roll back the tape of our own life, we can always "Rewind, be kind."

How to Deal

1. Rewind, by naming a past experience that you blame yourself for and that still impacts you today. Maybe you think about it, images

of it pop up in your head sometimes, or you dream about it—something like blaming yourself for not getting a job.

2. Write out the *unkind* interpretation of this experience. Something like, *I blew the job interview.*
3. Generate a new interpretation about yourself and that experience—a kind, loving, self-compassionate, self-forgiving, or self-exonerating thought. Something like, *I did the best I could during the interview. I was nervous, but anyone would be. I actually had some great moments. They probably just found a better fit.*
4. Take a few moments to sit with this new interpretation of yourself and your past experience. Repeat the new thought five to ten times.
5. Let yourself feel the warmth of the kind thought.
6. Use ratings before and after trying this skill if you want to track its usefulness more concretely.

14

Those Annoying GNATs

Struggle: persistent, annoying automatic thoughts

Picture yourself at a lovely picnic in the park—great weather, company, and food and drink. Then, slowly but surely, you realize gnats have descended on the picnic. They're buzzing, biting, and annoying you.

Just as we struggle to enjoy a picnic when gnats appear, we struggle to enjoy life when GNATs appear. Here, "GNATs" is one of our beloved acronyms, standing for "greedy negative automatic thoughts."

Automatic thoughts, as we've discussed, are unwanted, uninvited, and inaccurate statements that pop up in our head (Beck and Beck 2011; Tolin 2016). These thoughts strongly determine our experience of life by influencing our interpretation of ourselves, others, and the world.

The word "negative" describes the type of automatic thought we're having. We can have automatic thoughts that are positive, negative, or neutral. Negative automatic thoughts are the ones that make us feel not okay.

"Greedy" describes the negative automatic thoughts. While these thoughts aren't alive and sentient, we can think of them as having their own agenda: to spread like a virus, juicy rumor, or good meme. In this way, the negative automatic thoughts are "greedy"—just like the gnats that descend on our picnic for their own gain.

Skills like pooh-pooh *because it's true* (chapter 3) don't always work, because some automatic thoughts are GNATs: They're persistent and annoying, despite the tiny interventions we use against them. When this is the case, you can respond with several other skills.

First, *protect against GNATs* when you can. GNATs are more likely to descend on you when you're vulnerable and not thinking clearly. Things like keeping up on sleep, not using substances excessively, not engaging in physically draining activities, and not interacting with toxic people can help protect you from GNATs.

Next, *identify GNATs when they appear*. You're more likely to respond to GNATs effectively if you see they're flying around and then label them as GNATs. This requires you to be aware of your most common GNATs and of general GNATs that attack everyone.

Next, *try swatting GNATs away*. You can gesture like you're actually swatting gnats away, or you might tap your head to signify that you're trying to keep those GNATs moving along. Alternatively, you could swat verbally, saying something like, "Get outta here," or "I'm not paying attention to you."

Finally, *treat bites from GNATs* when they inevitably get you. Nobody can avoid GNATs altogether. When they bite, give yourself treatment—in this case, a combination of compassion for having the thoughts, and refutation of the thoughts. You might say, *It sucks that I'm having GNATs, but what they're saying isn't true.*

Life's not always a picnic. But, using these skills to prevent and respond to GNATs will help you enjoy many of life's moments without unnecessary distraction.

How to Deal

1. 1. Engage in daily self-care (see chapter 19) to protect against GNATs.
2. When your check-in checklist indicates you're not okay, ask, *What thoughts keep popping up in my head now?* Jot down two or three of your best guesses, and label these "GNATs."
3. Generate a response to these GNATs, e.g., a phrase intended to swat away or combat each GNAT.
4. Use other skills you've learned to respond to GNATs: Explain why you're having the thought, do self-compassion to generate sympathy for yourself, play Scooby-You to disprove the GNATs, or practice C you

later! to change the GNATs to something more accurate.
5. Keep a running list of your GNATs. Consult the list consistently so you know which GNATs to look for.

15

Strong but Wrong

Struggle: *feeling overwhelmed and wanting to make it stop*

Feeling overwhelmed is common because many circumstances can precipitate it. These include having strong urges to use a substance, consume food, or engage in other behaviors you may later regret; having intense, obsessive thoughts like needing to check that you locked the door or turned off the stove; and experiencing extreme emotions like fear, loneliness, shame, or anger. While these are very different experiences, they all can lead to feeling overwhelmed.

When we're feeling overwhelmed for any reason, the thing we may want most is to make it stop—to feel less distress than we do currently. It's completely understandable to want our suffering to abate and then to do things to abate it.

Simultaneously, it's useful to have a skill that teaches us we can sit with suffering. Strong but wrong is that skill. It's a skill that says: Despite our urges, thoughts, or emotions being *strong*, the notion that we have to act right now to reduce any associated discomfort is *wrong*.

Strong but wrong is an example of distress tolerance, a broader set of coping skills defined as anything you do to temporarily withstand—not reduce—your current discomfort (Linehan 1993; Tolin 2016). According to distress tolerance, you don't have to use the substance to stop the urge, check the stove to quiet the anxious thought, or seek out companionship to alleviate your loneliness. Instead, you can sit with—or tolerate—the distressing thing.

If you can tolerate your distress for a short time without responding to it, the strength of that distress will dissipate. Often in just a few minutes, you can go from extremely distressed to back to your un-distressed baseline (Beck and Beck 2011). And, you'll feel proud that you withstood the onslaught of distress instead of giving into it.

In addition to advocating that you don't immediately decrease distress when you're overwhelmed, strong but wrong serves another important purpose: It's a bridge to using other effective skills. In moments that you *do* want to decrease distress—which is totally human and fine, btw—strong but wrong gives you enough clarity to access and leverage those other skills.

Such skills are referenced in this book and include responding to negative thoughts with evidence-based thinking (chapters 3, 6, 11, 27), healthily shifting focus from whatever's distressing (chapters 10, 23, 32), and other creative ways to navigate an overwhelming experience (chapters 20, 29, 33, 38, 41, 45).

The strong urges, thoughts, and emotions you have are completely valid. Feeling overwhelmed by these things is equally valid. But the notion that you have to respond immediately to make these uncomfortable things go away, is not.

Prove that you're stronger than even your strongest urges, thoughts, and emotions—by temporarily tolerating the distress they create.

How to Deal

1. Make a list of urges, thoughts, and emotions that feel strong and that dictate you respond immediately.
2. Write out a response to each, using "strong but wrong" language in your response. For example, "The thought *I should check that I locked the door* is strong, but it's wrong. Every time I've checked it in the past, it's already been locked." Or, "My fear right now is intense, but that doesn't mean I have to do something to make it go away."
3. Add another, reinforcing phrase to each response—something like, "Each time I tolerate the urge to smoke instead of giving

into it, I'm proving that I'm stronger than the urge itself."
4. Track your successes so that over time you can see how many times you've successfully tolerated distress.
5. When you want to decrease distress instead of tolerate it, use strong but wrong first, and then other skills from the book afterward.

16

Failing Feelings

Struggle: *failure*

Failure can make us feel all the bad things: disappointed, depressed, angry, inferior, ashamed, regretful—the list goes on.

Yet, failure is inevitable. Nobody always succeeds, just like nobody's always okay. Whether it's a macro-level failure like losing big money, forgetting our lines on opening night, or not passing an important test, or a micro-level failure, like forgetting someone's name, killing a plant, or missing our kid's recital, failure finds us.

How can we process all the negativity that failure brings, live our daily lives, and somehow generate optimism for the future?

Because failure can hit us so hard, a multifaceted response is recommended.

First, feel what you feel. Your emotional response to failure is legit. Give yourself moments to cry, complain, and contemplate what you could've done better. This is partly how we learn from failures and do better next time.

Next, compartmentalize the failure by specifying what you failed (Tolin 2016). You're not a failure at life—whatever that means. You may have been unsuccessful in one endeavor, and that hurts deeply. But remind yourself that the failure was singular. Doing so may modulate your emotional reaction so it's more commensurate to the singular failure.

Related to that, separate process from outcome. Perceived failure frequently relates to not achieving an outcome: winning the game, passing the test, getting a date for the party. Absent from this interpretation is the process that preceded the failed endpoint. You might say, *The outcome sucked, but what about the process was good?* There's usually something to celebrate about the process that preceded the failure.

Visualizing your future self being happy can help with present failures. As hard as failure hits us, the truth is that after time passes—days, weeks, months, or years—many failures disappear from the bank of experiences that affect us day-to-day. Visualizing yourself in the future—when your current failure is no longer a palpable cognitive and emotional experience—can relieve the pangs of that current failure.

Some current failures even lead to future positive experiences. I've had many clients who once understandably perceived failed romantic relationships to be apocalyptic. But sometime later, they found an unprecedentedly deep joy in being single or with another partner(s). Keeping this in mind can transform your current hopelessness to hopefulness for the future.

Change "failure" to "perceived failure"—a quick cognitive and linguistic tweak that can help you interrogate and critique the interpretation that you failed. Who says or thinks you failed? Often, we think others are judging us for failure, but they don't think we failed at all! Reminding ourselves that *I'm being hard on myself; other people wouldn't perceive this as failure* can change our perception of failure to something more sympathetic.

And finally, doing self-compassion (chapter 9), practicing self-care (chapter 19), and taking an UPR (chapter 43) are also suggested strategies. These can give you a much-needed boost during your dark failure time.

Failure is like struggle more broadly, in that because it's inevitable, how we respond to it is important. Responding to failure effectively is a learnable skill set with meaningful payoffs, such as resilience and enduring self-love.

How to Deal

1. Name a failure that's stuck with you.
2. Rate how distressed you are by this failure currently, using a scale of your choice.
3. Pick your favorite strategy from above and apply it to this failure for one or two weeks. Then, rerate your current distress from the failure.

4. TEAPOT on repeat—applying the various skills above to the original or other failures.
5. Jot down the most useful skills in an easily accessible place. Consult this list during acute times of perceived failure.

17

Make Conditions, Not Decisions

Struggle: *making a tough decision*

Each day, immediately when we wake up, we hop aboard the decision train. And we ride that train all day. From morning to night, we're constantly deciding things: what to eat, what song or podcast to listen to, what work task to do next, when to pick up the kids, can I afford that, will I call that guy back, what time should I go to bed?

Sometimes you're able to make quick and confident decisions about things. When that's the case, great—go for it! When you can't make decisions easily, it can have consequences ranging from "slightly annoying" to "debilitating." In these latter cases, ease the burden of decision making by not making a decision at all. Instead, make conditions.

Making conditions is a two-step process. For step 1, pick out a few values related to the decision that are important to you (Barlow 2021; Hayes 2011). Broadly, values are the things that matter to you. For step 2, for each value articulate conditions under which you'd go either way on your decision. Use "If X, then Y" statements, with X being the condition, and Y being the decision.

Let's say you're deciding whether to apply for a new job. For step 1, pick out job-related values that matter to you—maybe salary, time off, and happiness. For step 2, your values-based conditional statements might be:

Salary: "*If* I don't get a cost-of-living raise this year, *then* I'll apply for a new job."

Time off: "*If* I get an extra paid week of vacation, *then* I'll stay at my current job."

Happiness: "*If* I'm not happier at work within three months, *then* I'll apply for a new job."

Implicit in each condition is a second, opposite condition. For example, "*If* I do get a cost-of-living raise this year, *then* I won't apply for a new job."

Making effective conditions is important because it sets you up to make your decision confidently. To make effective conditions, I recommend a few tips.

First, add a time component to each condition. That way, you have a finite assessment period. The "this year" in our salary condition is an example.

Second, make around two or three conditions for each decision, as we did above. This is a manageable amount so you're not trying to track too many moving parts simultaneously.

Finally, as you assess whether your conditions are met, use numbers or categories to rate and track things. For your condition about being happier at work, you might rate how happy you are at the end of each week using your favorite rating scale. This will give you some clear, concrete data to work with.

Making conditions is empowering because you're choosing what's most important to focus on when making a decision. Importantly, making conditions for a decision takes some pressure off making the decision itself. That's because when you make conditions for the decision, you set up the decision to make itself.

How to Deal

1. Identify a current decision you're struggling to make. (If you don't have one, keep this skill in your pocket for later.)
2. When such a decision pops up, pick two or three values related to the decision that are important to you.
3. Using the tips above, create an "*If* (condition), *then* (decision)" for each value.
4. Assess each condition after its time component expires.
5. Let the results of your assessment make the decision for you.

18

Be Your BFF, Not Your Bully

Struggle: *self-critical self-talk*

Self-talk is the way you talk to yourself, either out loud or inside your head. Your self-talk strongly influences how you experience life.

For example, negative self-talk—talking to yourself critically and harshly—is like having a bully in your head. If you stub your toe, the inner bully might say, *You're such an idiot!* If you make a mistake, the inner bully might mock you, *Good job, loser.* Even if you do something good, the inner bully might diminish it, *That's not good enough.*

These bullying words are called "negative self-talk" (Burnett 1996), and they're a main reason we can be hard on ourselves.

The opposite of bullying yourself with negative self-talk is being your own BFF with positive self-talk. "BFF" means "best friend forever," and being your own BFF means talking to yourself like you would talk to your best friend—which for many of us, is nicer than how we talk to ourselves.

Positive self-talk is the primary tool you can use to be your own BFF. If you stubbed your toe, your inner BFF could say, *Oh no! Are you okay? Let's check. Yes, you're okay.* If you make a mistake, your inner BFF might say, *No problem, nobody's perfect, you'll get it right next time.* And when you do something good, your inner BFF would say sincerely, *Great job!*

Being your own BFF takes a few steps: becoming aware of the inner bully, flipping the content of the bullying thoughts to create positive self-talk, and actively practicing positive self-talk.

To increase your awareness of the inner bully, you can jot down some of your most common self-critical thoughts; then, keep your antennae up for these. Some people even use a bell, an app with sound, or something else with sound. They'll ring the bell every time they catch the inner bully. This helps the fleeting but damaging bully thoughts "take shape," which makes them easier to notice, grab onto, and intervene on.

Next, you can flip the content of the bullying thoughts to generate positive self-talk. For example, *You're a failure* can be flipped to *You're a success*. If you have trouble flipping the bullying thought to something fully positive, you can aim for something neutral. For example, if you don't totally believe that *You're a success*, you can say, *You're not a failure* or *You're alright*.

The final step is to actively practice positive self-talk. For example, you can write down inner BFF thoughts on sticky notes and stick them to your bedroom mirror so you see them often. Whatever it takes to get positive self-talk in your head, that's what you can do for this step.

Everyone deserves a BFF—someone who supports you, cheers you on, and reminds you that you're pretty great. Why not be that friend to yourself? Positive self-talk is the mechanism that can help you get there.

How to Deal

1. Write down five to ten examples of your own negative self-talk. This may go quickly, or it may take you a few days to build this list.
2. Review these, searching for any themes. Perhaps a theme in *when* they occur, like right before work. Or a theme in their *content*, like they're all about your physical appearance. Use this knowledge to beware of negative self-talk at specific times or on specific topics.
3. For each of the negative self-talk thoughts, generate a positive or neutral self-talk alternative. To do this, state the opposite of the negative self-talk phrase. Or ask, *What would I say to my BFF? What would*

my BFF say to me? Write down these new, positive or neutral self-talk phrases.
4. Practice using these new phrases, by writing them down repeatedly, saying them out loud repeatedly, thinking them repeatedly, etc. The goal here is repetition, to facilitate training your brain to use positive self-talk.
5. If you'd like, use ratings to track your levels of negative and positive self-talk more concretely.

19

Put the Self in Self-Care

Struggle: *taking care of yourself*

Nowadays, the term "self-care" seems omnipresent. Defining what "self-care" means to you, and then doing it, are skills that will help you when you're not okay.

I'll offer my definition of "self-care:" any actions you take to promote your mental or physical well-being. But as you can see, my definition is vague. That's why it's important for each of us to define what self-care means to us.

There are few constraints to how you can define "self-care." The first is that self-care probably doesn't significantly damage your or anyone else's health. If you think self-care is drinking excessively or sending death threats to your nemesis, you're probably practicing something else—maybe avoidance or revenge.

Self-care also likely shouldn't prohibit you from executing other personal goals—things like being a good parent, partner, or friend. If so, you might be practicing escapism instead of self-care.

Some common forms of self-care reported by my clients include exercising, reading, cooking, sleeping, creating, thrifting, playing video games, dancing, and connecting with loved ones. But I encourage you to think deeply about what uniquely fills your tank.

First, reflect on what makes you feel more relaxed, happy, and empowered and less stressed, sad, and rueful. Next, create time to engage in those activities—even if briefly. I suggest to clients that they make as much time for self-care as they do for a therapy session, work meeting, or errand—aka at least an hour weekly.

Everyone has barriers to practicing self-care—work, relationships, life being life. That's why self-care gets a chapter in this book—it's a skill to acquire, practice, and incorporate into your life, even as life keeps lifing.

How to Deal

1. Make a list of self-care activities you've done, or currently do, that bring you joy, reduce stress, and make you feel most like yourself.
2. Pick one or two of these that are easiest to incorporate into your current schedule and life.
3. Find about an hour each week to do these things, even if that means something like ten minutes each day.
4. Use rating scales to assess whether practicing self-care helps, e.g., improves mood, confidence, self-love. Track this data

over time, noting which self-care activities consistently produce positive outcomes.
5. Be open to adding new self-care activities as you learn more about yourself and change your definition of self-care.

20

Thank the Crank

Struggle: *responding to negative emotions*

Negative emotions can make us feel conflicted, unstable, and lost. They can override rational thinking and remind us of our past pain and trauma. They can hit so hard that we disconnect from the world around us.

So, what can we do when negative emotions appear?

Not to be glib, but I suggest a straightforward and consistent response: *Thank them.*

Literally—either in your head, out loud, or both—say, "Thank you, _____." The blank here represents whatever the emotion is. I use "crank," for "cranky," because it creates a memorable, rhyming name for the skill. But I suggest you thank all your emotions—elation, fear, disappointment, jealousy, etc.

Why thank your emotions? Because they're messengers. Emotions are our body's way of telling us what's going on inside—specifically the internal biological, physiological, and neural experiences we're having. The emotions we feel are manifestations of that internal experience.

For example, if we feel fear, it's because of a specific combination of activation of the brain and nervous system, and release of neurotransmitters and stress-related hormones (LeDoux 2012).

Emotions can be overwhelming, but thanking them can reduce this overwhelm in several ways.

First, thanking our emotions is a calming, soothing way to respond to our body and brain. Much more calming and soothing than, say, berating ourselves for feeling a certain way.

Next, it helps center ourselves and connect to the rational, logical part of our brain. This is because the act of thinking about an emotion, labeling it with a word, and then saying thank you to it requires our rational, logical brain. Activating the logical part of our brain is a great way to deactivate our emotional brain, even just a little.

Thanking our emotions also can help us understand our thoughts and current situation better. We can ask ourselves, *What was I thinking right before feeling cranky?* or *What in the environment just made me fearful?* Having this contextual knowledge is empowering and can help us feel in control.

It's okay if you're feeling hesitant or doubtful about thanking your emotions. In that case, you can start practicing this new skill set by thanking that hesitancy and doubt. Those emotions are sending you a message about where you're at with this idea.

How to Deal

1. Use check-in checklists, or any form of self-monitoring, to track what emotions you're feeling throughout the day. Maybe you write down, or type on your phone, what emotion you're feeling three times daily for a week.
2. Once you're in this habit, you can start adding the "thank you" after each emotion you identify feeling. For example, "Thank you, Crank!"
3. Add a sentence to the "Thank you, _____" from step #2—a sentence that compassionately interprets *why* the emotion is being felt. For example, "Thank you, Crank! I probably feel this way because I'm still mad at my partner for what they said this morning."
4. Consider leaning into your original emotion. You *can* feel cranky if you want to, or if you think it's justified.
5. Alternatively, you can counter the emotion by generating thoughts, memories, and behaviors that evoke the opposite emotion. If you feel cranky, you might think, *I'm grateful for my partner*, you might remember a relaxing vacation, or you might take some deep breaths to relax.

21

That's So Meta(phor)

Struggle: *rigid thinking*

Sometimes we can get stuck in how we see ourselves and the world. We rigidly think we are who we are, never to change: *That's just who I am,* or *I'm a (loser, failure, piece of shit).* Similarly, we think the world is the way it is, never to be anything different: *It is how it is,* or *That's how things work.*

While it's true that some things don't change, such rigid thinking about ourselves and the world can make us feel depressed, hopeless, and trapped.

Metaphors are used by CBT (Tolin 2016), ACT (Hayes et al. 2011), and other therapies to facilitate the opposite of rigid thinking: psychological flexibility. Metaphors both help you see yourself in different ways and teach you that you can be *the* stable, consistent part of your experiences. This combination allows you to be flexible in how you see yourself, while building confidence in maintaining your strength and stability across situations.

To illustrate this point, let's review three useful metaphors that aim to accomplish both goals (Hayes et al. 2011). Read each of these slowly, pausing during each to visualize yourself as the thing. After each metaphor, reflect on whether the metaphor helped you see yourself differently than you do now, but always as the stable force in a world of hustle, bustle, and change.

You're an anchor. You're stable, still, hefty, and sitting calmly at the bottom of the ocean. A rope attached to you trails upward to the water's surface, where it's connected to a large ship. The world around you moves: Fish swim by. The rope constantly undulates underwater. Passengers on the ship above flutter with activity. Nearby ships' passengers similarly flutter. Birds fly around the ships. There is endless activity around you, but you remain the same: stable, still, unbothered, always tethered.

Not very nautical? How about...

You're a chessboard. You're an unchanging game board upon which infinite games are played. The chess pieces are used differently each game. There are new players and a new winner each game. No two games are ever the same. You—the chessboard—are neutral, unaffected by the previous games and their outcomes. Everything around you changes, but you are the calming, given, constant of the game.

Not into chess? Perhaps then...

You're the sun. You're the center of the universe. You're the source of light and life for us all. You're bright, powerful, and timeless. Your strength, energy, and capabilities are unmatched.

You're stationary, while the planets, their moons, and the stars all revolve around you. You move very little, while the gravity inside you is strong enough to move all other things.

Once you can see yourself in different ways—but as always stable—you'll likely be more accepting, self-assured, and psychologically flexible. You can apply this flexibility to thoughts about yourself and the world around you—being open to various iterations of each instead of rigidly seeing things in a specific way.

So, anchors aweigh, checkmate, and shine brightly.

How to Deal

1. Review the anchor, chessboard, and sun metaphors daily for two or three weeks. I recommend both reading and visualizing them.
2. Create your own metaphor with the same themes. Read and visualize that daily also.
3. Simultaneously, build a list of your own rigid thoughts about yourself and the world, by identifying and noting them as they pop up.
4. Keep reading and visualizing the metaphors, assessing over time if your relationship to these rigid thoughts changes as you connect more deeply to the metaphors.

22

Mirror, Mirror

Struggle: *communicating*

Sometimes it's hard to listen and respond effectively to others because internally we start reacting to what they say. Our thoughts race, our physiology activates, and we feel the feelings elicited by their words—including, and especially, defensiveness.

It can be difficult to respond effectively to others during any conversation, but in my personal and professional experience, it's hardest when receiving constructive feedback; when discussing sensitive topics, like finances, sex, and intimacy; and when talking to someone who's mistreated you in the past.

For as multifaceted as these moments are, the skill I recommend to help sounds simple: empathically reflecting back the emotion that's being communicated to you (Rogers 1957; Sharf 2015)—just like a mirror reflects what it sees.

Using mirror, mirror can ground you when someone's communicating with you, and your body and brain start to take flight.

This skill has two broad steps: Listen and respond. The listening portion necessitates that you focus on the words being said to you—so you can catch what *emotion* is being communicated.

This relates to something called "mentalizing"—when you realize someone is experiencing the moment differently than you and when you put yourself in their shoes to understand their experience of the moment (Bateman and Fonagy 2012). This empathic exercise can decrease your emotional and physiological activation, because you're focusing on understanding someone else's emotional experience, not yours.

The response portion challenges you to put into words what you think the person is feeling—things like, "You're really frustrated with me." You may include a gentle opening phrase like "I'm hearing that..." or "It sounds like..."

Additionally, you can include nonemotional words to provide context, e.g., "You're really frustrated with me because I didn't take out the trash despite saying I would." Both skills—reflecting back the speaker's emotion and paraphrasing what they're saying to you—relate to building positive relationships (Gamble and Coupland 2023).

You may not reflect someone else's emotion accurately—that totally happens. If so, you can try again or ask the person to correct you by telling you what they're feeling. This type of exchange can help whomever you're communicating with feel like you want to understand them, which can foster closeness.

And if you're currently thinking, *But when do I get to talk about my own feelings?*—good question. Usually, after you successfully reflect someone else's emotions, you create a space for sharing your own. And because using the mirror, mirror skill can decrease your own activation, if you share your emotions after using the skill, you may do so more calmly, clearly, and effectively.

Use this skill to make others feel heard and felt, and also to keep yourself calm when something difficult is being communicated to you.

How to Deal

1. Build your emotion vocabulary so you have at least several emotion words to choose from as you reflect. Even a simple online search of "common emotions" can help.
2. Generate a few go-to reflection phrases with others, e.g., "You feel _____ right now," or "I feel your _____ with you," filling in the blank with the emotion you're feeling from whomever you're talking to.
3. Practice using these phrases with low-stakes people in your life, during low-stakes situations—like a good friend you rarely argue with, when discussing how your days went.

4. When you're more confident in using this skill, try it out during higher-stakes situations—when you're receiving feedback at work, when your partner is opening up to you, etc.

23
Look Over There!

Struggle: *being stuck in an emotional funk*

RuPaul's Drag Race fans will recall Jaida Essence Hall's hallmark line, "Look over there!" She used it while playing a politician during a staged debate, suggesting that politicians often distract constituents instead of responding to them. Jaida not only won her season, but also gave us a strategy for when we're stuck in an emotional funk.

We've all been there. When we feel sad, anxious, or depressed for hours, days, or weeks. Those times are dark, made darker because they can feel impossible to get out of.

"Look over there!" is essentially a prompt you can give yourself to initiate distraction from your current emotional state.

Broadly, distraction techniques give our bodies and brains a break from constant, soul-sucking emotions. Specifically, distraction redirects our attention to a new stimulus. This helps alleviate our emotional funk in two ways: First, we reawaken our body to be sharp, alert, and ready for the next thing. Second, because attention is highly related to emotion (Tolin 2016), our emotions can shift when we shift our attention. Basically, as shown by research on something called "selective attention," where our attention goes, our emotions often go (Wadlinger and Isaacowitz 2011).

This is important information for those stuck in an emotional funk. Most of us can't just make ourselves feel a new, happier emotion. Thus, developing skills to change emotions is key to getting out of ruts.

"Look over there!" is a phrase that pulls our attention to something new. If we focus hard enough on that something new, likely our emotions will go there—such that we start feeling emotions associated with the new thing we're focusing on, not the original thing.

Distraction techniques can be verbal, like "Look over there!" Or, they can be behavioral. Behavioral distraction techniques include leaving whatever space you're in or starting a new activity that demands your attention.

Behavioral distractions are best time-limited so you don't risk falling into a funk while doing those. For example, playing video games as a behavioral distraction can be useful, but if you do it for hours, that may become your new funk.

As another caveat: Try distraction techniques that you're confident will be positive. For example, don't distract yourself by scrolling through social media if you know that doing so can bring you down.

Some people might think distraction techniques are ineffective. After all, they're not really addressing the core problem. They're just diverting our attention away from the problem temporarily. Even if we forget about the problem for a few minutes, it's still there.

And that's exactly why they're useful.

Yes, even if we use distraction techniques, the original problem will still be there. But your body and brain deserve a break from feeling bad. Distraction techniques pull your attention away from the problem, bring your emotions with it, and give you that well-deserved break.

And often, that break from the funk can be the spark you need to de-funk yourself longer term.

How to Deal

1. Use your past experiences and current insight to make a list of positive distraction techniques that could work for you. Broadly, the distraction can be a thought, phrase, activity, or location.
2. Make parameters for these distraction techniques, e.g., "for thirty minutes," "two times per week max," etc.
3. Next time you're in a funk, try one of your distraction techniques to shift your attention to something new.
4. Assess whether that brief period of distraction relates to feeling less funk-y. If

not, try a different distraction technique from your list.
5. If you feel less funk-y, capitalize by engaging in a nondistraction activity that is more deeply meaningful or joyful. (This last step aims to facilitate you getting out of the funk more enduringly.)

24

Set Your Alarm and Your Intention

Struggle: *starting new habits*

Set yourself up for success with two skills in which you *set* something else.

The first is your alarm—likely on your phone or electronic calendar. Using *periodic prompts* is a simple but often effective strategy that can help cue you to engage in new habits you're trying to adopt (Neff and Fry 2009). Virtually nobody can just successfully start new habits; instead, most of us reasonably need, and benefit from, reminders to do the new thing.

This new thing can be a behavior, thought, or anything else. Behaviors, such as eating a midday snack to keep your energy up or taking several deep breaths to relax before going to sleep. Thoughts, such as, *I'm loved, valued, and worthy,* or *Whatever I'm doing right now, I can do it well.* Anything else, such as a visualization practice or a prompt to write down one thing you're grateful for.

Basically, whatever new thing you're trying to incorporate into your life to improve your mental or physical health, an alarm can prompt you to do that thing, and may help you eventually automatize that thing into your daily life (Neff and Fry 2009). In other words, setting your alarm is both a tiny intervention and an effective strategy to use *while* doing the "practice over time" piece of TEAPOT.

Intentions are the second thing you can set that can facilitate new behavior (Ajzen 1991; Barlow 2021). By "intentions," I mean any desire or goal you have within a period of time. You can set an intention for the day, maybe "Compliment my romantic partner today," or "Paint for two hours today." Alternatively, you can set your intention for a specific moment, e.g., "Enjoy this phone call with my mom," or "Listen to my child as they tell me about their homework," or "Accelerate the golf club as I swing through."

One notable caveat is to set these things, but with flexibility. We're not looking to set "commands" for ourselves. Setting alarms and intentions are not meant to be overly strict exercises. Instead, they're best incorporated with the self-compassionate understanding that we also want to fully participate in life, and that such participation sometimes takes precedence over the alarm or intention we set previously.

So, aim to balance holding yourself accountable when you set an alarm or intention, with being flexible with yourself if you don't execute 100 percent of the time.

How to Deal

1. Start small here by setting one alarm, once a day, for one behavioral, cognitive, or other thing. Try this every day for a week. Assess whether you engage in your desired behavior, thought, or other thing more frequently than when you don't set the alarm.
2. Next, start adding intentions—either to your day or to moments in your day. They're usually short, something like, "I'm going to focus on myself instead of others," or "I'm going to appreciate the nice weather."
3. You can combine the setting of alarms and intentions by, for example, setting an alarm with an attached reminder of your intention. You can set an alarm for 5:00p.m. with the reminder, "End the work day and have a relaxing evening with the family, free of thoughts from work."

25

The Blame Game

Struggle: *blaming yourself*

We've all blamed ourselves for things—mistakes we've made, failed relationships, climate change, etc. Blaming ourselves can be especially easy when we're already feeling sadness, anger, or grief.

Sometimes it can be useful to assess and take responsibility for your contribution to things that didn't go right.

But for now, I'm asking you to try something else: To play *the blame game*. Specifically, to blame everyone else, and everything else, for you not being okay.

Seriously, give it a try.

It can be liberating, empowering, and just plain accurate to note that often, your problems can be blamed on other people and things.

Need some help with where to start? Here's a sincere, nonexhaustive list of people and things to blame for your problems.

***

Blame everyone from your past who fucked you up. Blame your parents for neglecting you, your siblings for mistreating you, and your teachers for not calling on you when you raised your hand. Blame your bullies for ridiculing you just for being you. Blame anyone who made you feel small, wrong, and different.

Blame the mold in your childhood home for feeling so sick all the time now. Blame smog, pollution, dust, and pollen for making it hard to breathe. Blame the city where you grew up for not having enough public transportation, grocery stores, and libraries to support your development. Blame the bad health care providers you've had, who have lacked empathy and who have dismissed your health concerns. Blame your boss, who's made your life a living hell. Blame ableist architecture that makes it hard to get into buildings. Blame gender reveal parties, which are incorrectly named and perpetuate the false gender binary. Blame forms and policies that are written only in English when they know non-English speakers use them. Blame ageism for making you feel inferior just because you've lived. Blame organized religion for making you feel like a sinner for being born, drinking alcohol, and having sex.

Blame the government, for everything. Blame politicians for ignoring your needs and serving themselves instead of their constituents. Blame every racist president we've had, starting with George Washington. Blame the explicitly racist country they've created. Blame colonialism and the colonizers, who have degraded your culture.

Blame imperialism for the unnecessary war, death, and trauma it's caused. Blame the patriarchy for oppressing you. Blame the profit-driven health care system whose goal is clearly not you being healthy. Blame capitalism, which tells you you're not working hard enough. Blame everything that's not on this list but should be. Blame me.

***

Sure, you've done some things that you can work on in the future. But for now, let's acknowledge the people and things that have—purposely or accidentally—colluded to make you not okay. These people and things deserve the blame.

Taking time to give them their fair share of blame can help free you from blaming yourself. That freedom can itself facilitate change, in that you'll likely be thinking more clearly, be more motivated, and be able to take change-related action.

How to Deal

1. List some past or present things you blame yourself for.
2. For each thing on your list, name a few people or things that you can reasonably blame, instead of yourself.
3. Write out why each person or thing is to blame.

4. Put it all together by reading it aloud, e.g., "I blame X for _____ because X did _____."

5. Later, whenever you want, you can take ownership of what you've contributed to the things you currently blame yourself for. But, always keep this exercise in mind when the self-blame flares up.

26

Let's Get Visual, Visual

Struggle: *your thoughts holding you back from change*

Have you ever wanted to make a change, but negative thoughts kept you stuck where you are? Maybe you want to learn to play guitar, but each time you start the process, your self-critical thoughts say, *Don't bother; you'll never be good.* These thoughts can be stressful and can hold us back from being who we want to be.

When we're caught in these negative thinking loops, the left side of our brain—the side more associated with language—is likely hyperactive, pumping out thought after self-critical thought. To counter that left-brain hyperactivity, try activating the right side of your brain—the side that's more activated when we do things like visualize, imagine, and dream (Gabel 1988).

Visualization and related techniques that activate the right brain can have multiple benefits. Broadly, such techniques can decrease language-based, negative thoughts from the left brain. Visualization of calming things also can promote relaxation. And, visualizing ourselves doing something can increase motivation to do that something (Rennie, Harris, and Webb 2014), in part because we're creating a visual road map to follow.

In terms of what to visualize, you've got options. You can visualize yourself *accomplishing a goal*. This can increase your motivation for and confidence in accomplishing that goal. Many professional athletes and performers use visualization as part of their training, specifically visualizing themselves winning big tournaments, performing well in key moments, etc.

If it's tough to visualize yourself fully accomplishing a goal, you can visualize yourself *completing steps toward a goal*. To do this, break down the ultimate goal into multiple steps, and imagine yourself doing each step. This can help make reaching the ultimate goal seem easier and more approachable by answering the question, What do I *do* to accomplish that goal?

You could visualize your thoughts themselves, *turning them into images*. This can give your thoughts shape, which may make them less intimidating and help you respond to them. For example, a former client visualized their nagging, pejorative thoughts to be coming from a sassy, chain-smoking drag queen. This made the client chuckle, which helped them take the thoughts less seriously.

Finally, you could visualize things that promote *relaxation and calm*. Like when you close your eyes and imagine a peaceful beach scene, jungle oasis, or any soothing image.

As for how to visualize, it's like meditation and yoga insofar as it takes time to master. Truthfully, you may not be great at visualization at first. That's okay! I suggest being nonjudgmental as you inevitably practice visualization imperfectly.

To set yourself up for effective visualization, try minimizing distractions, like outside noise. Get very specific as you conjure up visualizations. Imagine the very smallest details so your visualization is precise. This will help down the road as you try to do the things you've been visualizing. Engage all your senses while visualizing, not just your visual system. This will help increase the robustness of your visualization. Some people like to narrate what they're visualizing. That's fine, as long as the words don't overpower the visual you're creating. Finally, incorporate TEAPOT on repeat as you figure out your own best way to visualize.

How to Deal

1. Identify a cognitive loop you're stuck in—when negative thoughts keep you from taking action you'd otherwise take.
2. Assess how "stuck" you are currently, using a scale of 1 (low) to 10 (high).
3. One by one, try each of the visualization options above, specifically visualizing yourself getting unstuck.

4. After each option, do another "stuck" assessment from #2.
5. Track which individual visualization options, or which combinations of options, help get you unstuck most effectively.

27
Convert Your CDs to MP3s

Struggle: *cognitive distortions*

I know compact discs aren't technically a thing anymore. But in CBT there's another type of CD—cognitive distortions. These CDs are thinking patterns—frequently comprised of automatic thoughts—that are generally untrue, negative, and not focused on the present moment (Beck and Beck 2011; Tolin 2016).

Like other negative thoughts we have, CDs can serve as pessimistic narrators of our life. That's why identifying which CDs play in our head, and then converting those CDs into more effective thoughts, can change our experience of ourselves and the world.

You'll see some CDs elsewhere in this book (chapters 35 and 44). Here's a list of some other common ones:

Fortune telling: Predicting negative things will happen in the future—like, *The person I'm on a date with will reject me if I ask them out again.*

Mind reading: Assuming others are thinking negative things—like, *I just know they're judging me.*

All or nothing: When we think of things in extremes—like, *It's now or never.*

Catastrophizing: When we make something big out of something little—like, *I'm getting fired because I made one mistake at work.*

Disqualifying the positive: When we focus on the negative and underemphasize the good stuff—like, *It doesn't matter that I succeeded 100 times before, because I didn't succeed this time.*

Negative filter: When something bad happens to us and then our subsequent thoughts are negative because of it—like if we have a rough morning, and then all day our thoughts are negative.

Emotional reasoning: When we feel strongly about something and then assume that feeling definitely reflects reality—like, *I feel anxious, so I just know something bad is gonna happen.*

Personalization: When we make things about us, even when they're not—like, *It's raining outside because of me.*

Labeling: When we call ourselves, or label ourselves with, mean names—like, *I'm a loser.*

After you've identified your most common CDs, you can try to convert them to more effective thoughts—something I call "MP3s."

Here, "MP3s" stands for thoughts that are *more plausible, more pleasant, and more present.* Each "MP" here counters one of the core characteristics of distorted thoughts.

More plausible thoughts correct the "untrue" nature of CDs. For example, changing the personalization thought *It's raining outside because of me* to a more plausible *It's raining outside because of clouds and the storm system.*

More pleasant thoughts correct the "negative" nature of CDs. For example, changing the labeling thought *I'm a loser* to a more pleasant *I'm likable, kind, and I bring a lot to the table.*

More present thoughts correct the "not focused on the present moment" nature of CDs. For example, changing the fortune-telling thought *The person I'm on a date with will reject me if I ask them out again* to the more present *The person isn't rejecting me now, so I'm going to have a good time.*

Converting your CDs to MP3s will help you regulate not only your thinking, but also your related emotions and behaviors. And more broadly, you'll feel more in control of the narratives that play in your head.

How to Deal

1. Review the list of CDs above. Pick a type of CD that's common for you.
2. Write out a specific example of this type of CD that you have.
3. Now, try to convert this CD to a MP3. Write out new thoughts that:
    a. provide accurate counter-evidence to the original thought (more plausible), and/or
    b. use words that are kinder and more positive than the original thought (more pleasant), and/or
    c. describe the current moment (more present).
4. TEAPOT on repeat with these. It takes time and effort to change the content of our thoughts, but it's possible, and comes with great rewards.

28

You Live, You Unlearn

Struggle: *breaking free from your past*

The phrase "You live, you learn" suggests that as you live life, shit happens—things like you're mistreated, relationships end, and you fail. These experiences are tough, but as a consolation prize, you learn lessons about life that help you down the road.

Indeed, growing up, we're learning lessons all the time—from parents/guardians, other family members, neighbors, teachers, the media. Some lessons are benevolent and generally accurate, like "I deserve love," and "Kindness begets kindness." However, sometimes we learn lessons that are untrue and damaging. Lessons like "I'm dumb," "Feeling stressed is normal," or "People can't be trusted."

Lessons like these, although perhaps reflective of our own experiences, don't generally reflect the world around us. Yet, because we've learned these lessons early in life, they can strongly influence how we think about ourselves, others, and the world; how we feel across various situations; and which behaviors we engage in.

But just as you learned these lessons, you can unlearn them. Moreover, you can replace these toxic lessons of the past—with more accurate, effective lessons.

To facilitate unlearning, the first step is to reflect on the potentially damaging, untrue lessons you've learned throughout your life. Ask yourself, "What did X teach me about life?" with X being anyone who's made a negative mark on you.

Alternatively, you could ask, "What did my past relationship with X teach me about life?" as past personal relationships are often the source of toxic life lessons that may not apply to everyone.

You also could pick five to ten early-life experiences that influenced you negatively growing up—things like switching schools, getting heartbroken, or worse—and then list what potential "lesson" you learned from each experience. Filling in the blanks in the following sentence may help: "When _____ happened, I 'learned' that _____."

The lessons you produce from this exercise could be interpreted as what CBT calls "core beliefs"—deep-seated thoughts about ourselves or the world that causally influence our experience of life (Beck and Beck 2011).

Once you've identified some potential toxic lessons you've learned, identify examples of counter-evidence to each. Scour your past and current experiences for examples of the toxic lesson being *untrue*. These pieces of counter-evidence are primarily going to be positive people, relationships, and experiences throughout your life.

To replace the old lessons with newer ones, try to cultivate current positive relationships and experiences in your life. Actively note when these provide you with a more benevolent, generally accurate lesson about other people and the world. Articulate the new lessons, something like, "People who care about me will stick around."

This can be challenging and time-consuming work. I suggest being patient and self-compassionate throughout.

That could even be one of your new lessons: *I can be patient and self-compassionate as I change for the better.*

How to Deal

1. Make a list of some toxic lessons you learned while growing up.
2. Give each toxic lesson a rating indicating how much you believe it now, using a scale of 1 (low) to 10 (high).
3. For lessons with high ratings, use the strategies above to unlearn and replace the lesson. TEAPOT on repeat may be useful here.
4. After some time, rerate how much you believe each lesson. We're aiming to get lower "belief" ratings as you practice unlearning the toxic lesson.

5. For extra practice, link each lesson to your current thoughts, emotions, and behaviors. What have you thought, felt, or done recently that could have been influenced by each lesson? Pay attention to these—specifically if they decrease in frequency or strength—as you try unlearning the toxic lesson.

29

Create Space

Struggle: *responding to stress*

Have you ever been going about your day, and then you hear a sound that's the same as your morning alarm? You may think, *I have to get up!*, your heart starts beating, and you feel anxious—like you have to get out of bed and start your day. This is an example of something very human—to react to a stressful stimulus in an automatic way.

Because this reaction is so automatic, you might struggle with how to respond effectively to it.

As a demonstration of this, if you're able, push together your thumb and your index finger so the fingerprint side of each of them is touching. If you do this and hold your hand up in front of your face, you should see that your two touching fingers have created an eye-like shape. Your thumb represents the stressful "stimulus," and your index finger represents your automatic "reaction." Try to hold these together until the end of the chapter.

When we put these fingers together—so that there's no space between them—it represents a "fusion" between the stressful stimulus and automatic reaction. "Fusion" here means that the two things are so tightly linked, they don't seem separate—even though they are. This fusion between stressful stimulus and automatic reaction makes us struggle to feel control and to respond to the stimulus how we want to (Luoma and Hayes 2003).

When we're experiencing this stimulus-reaction fusion, we can try to *create space* between them. Doing so will help us volitionally respond to the stimulus, instead of automatically react to it.

You've got options on how to create space between a stressful situation and your reaction. First, try to recognize you're caught in a fusion moment, and label it. You might say, "I'm fused." (Or, to pay homage to the 1990s cult film, you could say, "I'm dazed and fused.") Labeling these moments is important because it gives you a sense of awareness and control over what's happening.

Otherwise, you could take one or two deep breaths, which can create the effect of slowing down the moment. You could use a specific phrase or thought to help you feel in control, for example, *Hold on, I got this*. You could do something that interrupts the fusion, e.g., blinking five times slowly, or putting your thumb and index finger together, then pulling them apart. You might visualize something calming to relax your body and give yourself time to think more clearly.

In addition to my suggestions, ask yourself, "Based on what I know about myself, how can I create space?" Maybe it's with a personal joke you have, or by recollecting a specific memory, person, or phrase.

How much space are we aiming to create here? Not much at all. If you're a trooper and are still holding your thumb and index finger together, go ahead and pull them apart—your thumb downward and your index finger upward—*as little as you can* such that they're not touching, but they're *super close* to touching. That's how much space we're going for.

Creating just a little space between stimulus and reaction can give you enough time to respond more willfully and effectively.

How to Deal

1. Identify two or three common stressful stimuli from your past—thoughts, sounds, images, people—that have elicited automatic reactions.
2. Note the specific automatic reactions you have to each stimulus—thoughts, emotions, how your body feels, etc.
3. Write out these connections, e.g., "When _____ happens, my automatic reaction is _____."
4. Now list two or three ways you can "create space" between each stressful stimulus and automatic reaction.

5. The next time a stressful stimulus pops up, use your listed strategies to create space.
6. Use the space you just created to respond volitionally to the stimulus instead of react automatically.

30

Count Your ACEs

Struggle: *understanding past trauma*

Please note: This and the next chapter discuss early-life trauma. Thus, these chapters can hit harder than some others. Proceed only if you want to think about potential trauma you've experienced. If not, relax, do something nice for yourself, and take these next two chapters off.

"ACEs" is a new-ish acronym in medicine, psychology, public health, and other fields, standing for adverse childhood experiences (Felitti et al. 1998). ACEs are a form of trauma, which we can define as "something awful you experience that scrambles your thoughts and emotions, and that often leads to avoidance of triggering cues" (Barlow 2021).

Any kind of trauma—including ACEs—can both become embedded in you and trickle down into your current life. That's why knowing which ACEs you've experienced, and how many you've had in total, can help you understand and respond to any current trauma-related vulnerabilities. This chapter gives you the skill of counting your ACEs.

There are ten established ACEs currently, although certainly each of us could have experienced stressful, painful, or traumatic things growing up that aren't on the list. ACEs are divided into two categories—personal things you've experienced and what others around you have experienced.

Here they are:

Personal	Others
Physical abuse	Substance abuse or dependence in home
Sexual abuse	Domestic violence in home
Emotional abuse	Family member incarcerated
Physical neglect	Family member with mental illness
Emotional neglect	Separated parents or guardians

The idea is that each of us has an "ACEs score," which equals the number of events above that we experienced growing up. That's one point for each ACE, for up to ten total.

Most of us have at least one ACE (Merrick et al. 2019). As evidence that early-life trauma can affect us later, the more ACEs you've had growing up, the likelier you are to have later-life mental and physical health challenges—from anxiety and depression, to cancer and heart disease (Hughes et al. 2017).

You may be asking, "What do I do if I have ACEs?" or "How do I respond to a high ACEs score?" These are great questions with multifaceted answers. I'll provide a couple answers in the next chapter, but for now, one clear response to these questions is something like, "Love yourself."

No one deserves to experience traumatic things, and I'm sorry if you have. Let's take this moment to sit in self-love, to tell yourself that you didn't deserve your ACEs, and to give yourself sympathy for experiencing them.

How to Deal

1. Struggling with trauma can be taxing on our mental and physical health. You don't need to do ACEs-related work, at all or on your own. If you do want to do this work on your own, do it at a slow pace and always be open to hitting pause or stop.
2. If you've read the above and would like to try this exercise, calculate your ACEs score.
3. Whether your score is 1, 10, or anything in between, do self-compassion and practice self-care, in whatever forms are meaningful to you.
4. Start the next chapter if/when you want to learn other suggested responses to ACEs.

31

What to Do with Trauma

Struggle: *past trauma creeping into the present*

If/when you're ready, let's continue our discussion of ACEs and past trauma.

I've now introduced the concept of ACEs, you've calculated your ACEs score, and hopefully you've practiced self-love in a way that's meaningful to you. As a next step, this chapter provides two skills to help you respond to trauma more comprehensively.

The first skill encourages you to explore how past trauma may affect you in the present. I call this, "drawing the trauma through-line," from initial trauma to present day. By "through-line" here, I mean a reasonable, thematically related link from the past to the present. Drawing the trauma through-line and then responding to your present experience with understanding, compassion, and self-love can help minimize the pervasiveness of trauma's effects.

To give two personal ACEs examples: First, in second grade, I had a bully who frequently spat in my face. To this day, I'm kinda disgusted by the sight of saliva—even when I see, like, babies drooling. Second, in my home growing up, my father was loud and could become violent.

Nowadays, I become fearful and agitated when people start yelling—I've had to walk out of work meetings when I perceive someone becoming loud and aggressive.

In each of these examples, I can draw a through-line from the ACE I experienced in the past to the negative experience I have in the present.

If you're wondering, *Could my (aversive reaction to X now) be linked to (my past trauma related to X)?*, the answer is probably "at least a little."

While we can't go back and erase things like ACEs, we can practice strategies that help mitigate their impact on our lives today. The second skill in this chapter includes such strategies. I think of it as "when life deals you ACEs, play *CARDS*."

"CARDS" is an acronym including five strategies to use when coping with trauma. The C stands for "community," and it reminds us to seek out people we align with, share values with, and trust. My own research in Chicago has shown that community engagement can relate to reduced associations between ACEs and poor health (Woodward et al. 2021).

A is for "awareness," and it means to know your ACEs score, to be aware of present-day effects of trauma, and to accurately attribute some present-day challenges to past trauma. Awareness can be increased by educating yourself about trauma, doing regular check-in checklists with yourself about trauma specifically, and per above, drawing trauma through-lines.

R is for "release," and it refers to release of negative emotions related to your ACEs. I recommend generating a few strategies that allow you to release negative emotions, e.g., meditation, exercise, creative endeavors, talking to a loved one, individual or group therapy, etc.

D is for "deep breathing." When you have trauma-related thoughts, emotions, or physiological reactions, you can try stopping what you're doing for a few seconds and taking a few deep breaths. This can help you regulate your physiology, orient you to the current moment, and help you think more clearly (Tolin 2016).

Finally, the S stands for "self-compassion." It reminds you that your trauma wasn't your fault and to be kind toward yourself as you understand that ACEs and other trauma may still affect you now.

Use these two skills—drawing your trauma through-lines and playing CARDS with your ACEs—to understand how trauma affects you now and how to respond to it effectively.

How to Deal

1. You don't have to do any trauma-related work unless you're ready. If/when you're ready, proceed to #2.

2. Write out the following sentence and fill in the blanks as much as you want: "Because I experienced _____ in my past, I think/feel/act _____ now." Fill in the first blank with the ACE/trauma you experienced and the second blank with the current, unpleasant thing you struggle with—scary thoughts, strong emotions, avoiding something, etc.
3. Practice playing CARDS, assessing which of the strategies is most effective in reducing any cognitive, emotional, or behavioral dysregulation that may be associated with past trauma. Begin linking specific, effective CARDS strategies with specific types of dysregulation, e.g., "Use deep breathing when I have triggering memories." Or "Use community when I'm feeling emotionally overwhelmed."
4. If you have health care access, consider working with a mental health professional who can help you with structured exposure activities. These include things like telling the story of your trauma repeatedly until you gain a sense of control over the traumatic experience.

32

The WAIT-ing Game

Struggle: fixating on something negative

Sometimes we have thoughts that are negative, but they're also accurate. Things like, *I've gotten fired from my last three jobs.* Similarly, sometimes we're in a situation that is unpleasant, but we can't change it. Times like, being caught in the rain without an umbrella.

There's not really anything to challenge in the above examples. No amount of "evidence-based thinking" can change some circumstances. We need a different skill for these inevitable, unchangeable life moments.

The WAIT-ing game is a skill that reminds us that sometimes we just have to "wait" things out. "WAIT" is also an acronym for "What also is true?" It's helpful to ask this question during times of unavoidable discomfort, because it prompts us to shift our focus from the original uncomfortable stimulus to other thoughts we're thinking, emotions we're feeling, and behaviors we're engaging in.

That's the thing: At any one time, there are an infinite number of things that are true. Reminding ourselves of some of those *other* true things when we're uncomfortable can help reduce our discomfort.

The WAIT-ing game can be played in various situations—from being stuck in traffic, to having an insufferable coworker, to living life with health limitations. I use this skill personally when my health condition flares up and limits my mobility. On such days, I'll inevitably be sad that I can't do certain activities and frustrated that I'm pain. Recognizing that I can't make my body feel better by like, snapping my fingers, I think things like, *My body is having a bad day. I can't do everything I want to, and I'm in pain. But, what also is true?*

I generate whatever I can that's indeed true. Usually things like, *I'll do the things my body *will* let me do; Today can be a relaxing, sedentary day;* or more broadly, *I'm grateful that not every day is like this.* I'll also focus on environmental factors that bring me some joy, e.g., *The sandwich I just made tastes good,* or *The colors of the sunset tonight are beautiful.*

Playing the WAIT-ing game, plus the broader *Sometimes I just have to wait this out* reminder, never totally changes the situation. In my case, my mobility remains limited, I still feel pain, and I'm still sad and frustrated. But, playing the WAIT-ing game invariably ameliorates the situation a little.

I can't WAIT for you to try this skill!

How to Deal

1. Identify a current uncomfortable thought you're having, or uncomfortable situation you're in, that you can't successfully challenge or change.
2. Generate a thought related to waiting it out, something like, *This isn't great, but sometimes I just have to wait.* Repeat this as much as you want.
3. Ask yourself, "What also is true?" Provide as many responses as you can, using answers that are both true and more comforting than the current discomfort you're facing.
4. You can focus on just one of your answers or alternate between them—whichever brings you more temporary relief from the current discomfort.
5. When you think you've run out of responses to "What also is true?," challenge yourself to come up with a few more. There are always more things that are also true!

33

Give Life to Your Loss

Struggle: *grief*

Grief is one of life's cruelest, most universal struggles. We're all basically guaranteed to lose some people we love deeply and some things we cherish the most. What can we do when we're not okay because we're grieving a loss?

First, there's virtually no wrong way to grieve. As long as you're not harming yourself or others, not denying the reality of the loss, and able to eventually live life again, let yourself grieve in ways that are meaningful to you.

Beyond this axiom, there's something else to try while grieving: Give life to your loss. Grief is hard, among other reasons, because of the implicit finality of our loss. Whether it's a person, relationship, pet, career path, or dream we're pursuing, when these things are gone, it can be forever. We can assuage this sense of finality by giving continued life to that which is gone.

While the life of someone, something, or a pursuit may be over, the life given by that someone, something, or pursuit can continue. Whatever's been lost can continue to live on—through your words, actions, and continued invocation of them.

If your parent dies, they can live through you, e.g., as you parent your own children using the same values, words, and actions with your children as your parent did with you.

If your pet dies—maybe the pet you've had seemingly forever—they can live through you as you show love to future pets, people, plants, or things.

If someone ends a relationship with you, that relationship can live on as you implement the lessons learned from it; give your time, energy, and emotions to others; and if you choose, cultivate new relationships.

If you stop pursuing art to take a 9-to-5, your artist self can live on in future professional experiences as you bring that energy and perspective to the 9-to-5 spaces you now occupy.

In each case, something has indeed ceased to exist—and that really, deeply hurts. But, insofar as what's been lost has left an indelible and enduring mark on you—one that imbues your thoughts, feelings, behaviors, and remaining relationships—it's been lost a little less.

This skill also encourages you to interact with others as you grieve: Giving life to a loss is achieved best by invoking and spreading the memories, words, actions, and values of what's been lost to others. The more people you share these things with, the more life you give to whom or what's been lost.

Giving life to your loss won't resolve your grief, but it may help you cope with it.

How to Deal

1. Give yourself permission to grieve in any way that works for you.
2. If you're harming yourself or others, denying reality, or suffering endlessly, consider trying individual or group therapy or generally seeking support from others.
3. List some memories, words, actions, and values from whom or what's been lost. You can ask, "What about the person or thing do I want to live on through me?" You can do this step alone or with people you trust.
4. Identify specific parts of your life where you can invoke and use the things listed in #3.
5. Practice this invocation, while continually seeking support from others when needed.

34

Pause for Pride with a Praise Phrase

Struggle: *being proud of yourself*

How often do you feel pride compared to other, more negative emotions? If you're like me and most of my clients, pride is harder to come by than, say, sadness, guilt, worthlessness, and shame.

This is, unfortunately, unsurprising. We all face daily micro- and macro-level barriers to feeling pride. At the micro-level, we may be dealing with a critical boss, family members who belittle us, and our own self-doubt. At the macro-level, society tells us things like work harder, smile more, and look perfect.

Past experiences of critique also can be a barrier to feeling pride. Parents/guardians scolding us more than complimenting us, bullies ridiculing us frequently, or other meaningful or repeated experiences of critique—these past experiences can make it easier to now feel things like shame rather than pride. We may even hear the critical voices of our parents/guardians, bullies, or others in our heads throughout our day. Things like, "You idiot!" or some slur.

To combat such thoughts and more broadly to facilitate more frequent experiences of pride, I suggest developing a *praise phrase*—a few words intended to praise what you've done or who you are. Common praise phrases include "Great job with that," "That was very nice of me," and "I'm fucking amazing."

After you pause to think, say, or write down your praise phrase, take a beat to then feel the subsequent positive emotion—ideally, pride. It's important to both use the praise phrase and then reflect on how it makes you feel. Otherwise, the praise phrase may get swept under the rug, unable to permeate you with its positive effects.

After you pause, use a praise phrase, and feel pride, reflect on your experience of feeling pride: What thoughts do you have? How does it feel in your body? What resistance to pride do you experience?

Use TEAPOT on repeat with this skill to make it your own and to make it work for you. The ultimate goal is to work this skill into your routine so much that it becomes automatic.

Imagine a life in which pride is embedded into your daily routine, instead of things like critique, worthlessness, and guilt. This skill will help you get there.

How to Deal

1. Create a personal praise phrase—one that is meaningful to you and that is likely to make you feel good about yourself. Write it out somewhere and make it accessible.
2. For the next few days, try pausing each time you do something to be proud of—even seemingly small things, like brushing your teeth, sending an email, calling a friend.
3. If you have trouble with #2, set a daily alarm or daily email to be sent to yourself—to remind you to pause for pride with a praise phrase.
4. After you pause, say your praise phrase aloud. Look at the praise phrase as you say it—both saying and seeing the phrase repeatedly may facilitate automatizing it.
5. Take a few seconds to assess how this makes you feel emotionally, what thoughts you have, and how your body feels. Let pride sink it. Try to tell yourself, *This is how pride feels*.

35

The Challenge System

Struggle: *erroneous thoughts*

At the 2004 US Open, the greatest tennis player of all time—Serena Williams—was on the receiving end of multiple, egregiously bad line calls. She lost the match, and the tennis world would eventually apologize to her for the calls, and the loss.

In response to these epic errors, tennis broadly adopted "the challenge system." This system—now itself mostly phased out for a totally electronic system—permits players to contest a line call made by a lines person, and to see a slow-motion replay of the last ball landing.

You can use your own "challenge system," to check if your thoughts are like those infamous calls against Serena: erroneous. Erroneous thoughts could be automatic or not, and they commonly use strong or extreme language, make you feel crummy, or both.

To challenge your thought, use a version of slow-motion replay—specifically, play back the thought in your head. This will help you reexamine the thought, break it down word by word so you can examine each word's accuracy, and provide counter-evidence to it.

Let's say you have the thought *My friend calls me only when they need something.* Recognizing the "extreme" wording of this thought and that it leaves you feeling bad, you can challenge it.

Examining each word of the thought, you identify the word "only" as potentially extreme. Sure, your friend *often*, or even *frequently*, calls when they need something. But, as you play back recent times your friend's called, you remember they called last month just to ask how you were doing.

In this example, your playback revealed counter-evidence to the original thought. Recognizing the thought is erroneous, you now can correct the thought so it's error-free. Something like, *My friend frequently calls me when they need something, but they've also called to ask about me.*

I recommend tracking your successful challenges over time, nonjudgmentally noting common ways your thoughts are erroneous. Maybe your thoughts unnecessarily include the words "always" and "never." Or you often think, *I just know it*, even though you don't, in fact, know it. Or your thoughts tell you others are judging you, despite no evidence.

Over time, repeatedly identifying your erroneous thoughts, and then challenging them, will help you shift your thought content to be more error-free.

Sometimes a challenge is unsuccessful. This occurs when your playback indicates each word in the original thought was accurate, and you can't think of any legit counter-evidence to the thought.

For example, maybe you can't think of a single time your friend called to ask how you were doing. When this happens, assess how the original thought makes you feel. Feel that feeling, making room to do self-compassion because the thought is true.

Finally, consider whether you want to take any action related to your thought—in our example, perhaps talking to your friend about the friendship being one-sided.

How to Deal

1. Check in with yourself once daily for a week, recalling a thought from that day that seemed extreme, made you feel crummy, or both.
2. Play back the thought in your head (or write it out if you prefer to see it). Examine each word of the thought for errors.
3. Provide counter-evidence to the thought when possible.
4. If the challenge is successful, generate a new, error-free thought.

5. As you start catching extreme or negative thoughts in the moment, use this skill on them.
6. If the challenge is unsuccessful, consider any actions you might take to address the thought or situation.

36

What's the Delay?

Struggle: *feeling behind*

Have you ever felt behind compared to *others*—like you haven't developed core cognitive, emotional, or interpersonal competencies as fast as other people in your life? Or maybe you've felt behind compared to *yourself*—like you're proficient professionally and have great friendships, but struggle mightily with romantic relationships?

These experiences can leave us feeling delayed, as though we're waiting for ourselves to catch up.

While this phenomenon can apply to anyone, it's been reported most commonly by my clients who are LGBTQ+, are non-white, or have other minoritized identities; who have had enduring difficulties learning or paying attention; or who have experienced abuse or trauma.

I think of these delays as unsolidified skill sets—unsolidified because of early-life experiences that we had or didn't have. For example, if while growing up, we didn't get soothed when we were emotionally dysregulated, it may be challenging for us to modulate our own emotional dysregulation now. If we weren't taught critical thinking skills while growing up, we may be more gullible and naïve now. If we didn't have a close friend group or date others during high school and college, we may now feel unable to cultivate and maintain healthy relationships.

Identifying and catching up on our delays are key skills. You can usually identify your own delays by asking, *What's pretty much always been hard for me that seems easier for others?* Maybe your friends generally see the glass half full, while you see it half empty. Maybe your relatives are resilient when facing stress, but stress really keeps you down. Maybe your partner can usually say no to another drink at the end of the night, but you always say yes. Each of these is a potential delay you could identify and then catch up on.

To catch up on your delays, first, *be compassionate* that you have delays at all. Your delays aren't your fault. They're not punishments for something you did wrong.

Relatedly, try to *build insight* into where each delay came from. You can ask, *Why didn't I have the chance to develop the cognitive, emotional, or behavioral skill sets that others have?* Usually, delays occur because of outside factors, such as a lack of affirmation, resources, or opportunities—like if during childhood your family belittled and ridiculed you, nowadays you may struggle with self-confidence. Understanding your delay's origin can reduce self-blame for the delay.

Next, *be patient* as you catch up on your delay. This process takes time to address legitimately and fully. Thus, moving slowly while you catch up is normative, not blameworthy.

Pair this patience with *practicing* the skill sets you feel delayed on. This is when you're brave and put yourself out there—trying new things, thinking new thoughts, and cultivating new feelings.

Finally, *praise your effort* to catch up on your delay, even if you're not seeing progress. Broadly, be generous instead of stingy with the self-praise during this process.

How to Deal

1. Assess whether you have any meaningful cognitive, emotional, or behavioral delays, reflecting on what's always been hard for you but usually is easier for others.
2. If you feel stuck with this assessment, consult with trusted loved ones about their perception of what you struggle with.
3. Give yourself a baseline rating regarding where you're at with any delay. You can use a scale of 0 (no skill set, totally delayed) to 100 (full skill set, no delay).
4. Use the steps above to catch up on a delay.
5. Every month or so, reassess where you're at with the delay by giving yourself a new rating.

37

You Might Suck Too Much

Struggle: *should I take meds?*

Some of us are not okay because of persistent or severe symptoms—things like constant anxiety or very low mood. If you frequently find yourself in a funk, despite efforts to feel better, biology may be the explanation: Your body may be sucking up the stuff that makes you feel good, before the stuff has a chance to do its thing.

We all "suck" to some extent—each of our bodies continuously generates, releases, and "sucks up" infinitesimally small things, like neurotransmitters and hormones. They float around inside our body, strongly influencing things like mood and anxiety.

Serotonin is a really important one of these super small things: It relates to mood, anxiety, sleep, appetite, and more (Mohammad-Zadeh, Moses, and Gwaltney-Brant 2008).

When we have enough serotonin free-floating around in our body, we're likely to feel happy and calm. When we're feeling depressed or anxious, it may be because our body has "sucked" up the free-floating serotonin too quickly. It's like when you have an overactive Roomba that turns on and cleans your floor, even when you don't want it to.

I do have two good pieces of news. First, this "sucking" too much can be addressed by implementing many of the strategies in this book. You absolutely can influence the level of serotonin in your body with your thoughts, emotions, and behaviors. Second, "sucking" too much also can be addressed by prescription medication—specifically, medication that inhibits your serotonin-sucking Roomba.

These medications are called SSRIs: selective serotonin reuptake inhibitors. They prevent some free-floating serotonin from being sucked back up too quickly. This leaves serotonin floating in your body, to release its goodness. When experiencing persistent low mood or high anxiety, you might consider taking a SSRI to address these things.

For some people, finding the right SSRI improves their life significantly. For others, it helps a little bit. And for others, SSRIs don't work at all—or even can make things worse. So, trying SSRIs—or other medications—when you're struggling with persistent low mood or anxiety can be a challenging and long process. There are many SSRIs available, and the first or second one you try might not work for you.

If you're at all remotely interested in taking a SSRI for your mental health, and if you have access to health care, I recommend consulting with a general physician or psychiatric assistant. It's much better to get your info from them than online sources.

If you do start meds, you'll still want to use skills from this book. While some research questions the effectiveness of SSRIs (Jakobsen, Christian, and Gluud 2020), plenty of research says that for many people, SSRIs work (for example, Nutt 2000). Most commonly, research indicates a combination of meds and therapy-based skills like those in this book is the most effective approach to increase mood and reduce anxiety, across the lifespan (for example, Cuijpers et al. 2014).

That's why skills like the ones in this book are so important: Even if you take meds for your mental health, likely you'll "get a boost" from them. But the meds won't do all the work for you. Instead, primarily, the meds will make it easier to learn and implement the skills you're learning here.

How to Deal

1. Talk to a medical professional if you're experiencing persistent low mood or high anxiety, are considering taking a SSRI (or

other med) to address it, and have health care access.
2. Additionally, you can do research on SSRIs, their side effects, etc., as long as you use reputable sources—like peer-reviewed journal articles, instead of things like online threads.
3. If you're open to biological family members knowing that you're considering meds, assess whether they've taken meds for mental health. If they did and the meds worked for them, consider trying that med first (O'Reilly, Bogue, and Singh 1994).
4. For the first two to four weeks on a new med, assess whether you're having any negative side effects. If so, consider a new med. If not, keep taking the med and then for the next few weeks, assess for clinical effects—whether your symptoms are improving.
5. If you don't want to take meds, for whatever reason, that's fine! Focus instead on using the skills described here, building community, and self-care.

38

Aesop in Your Brain

Struggle: emotion overpowering reason

While chapter 29 discussed creating space between a stressful stimulus and your response, this chapter discusses something related, but different: any time your emotions dominate your experience.

Remember Aesop's story about the tortoise and the hare? Basically, two animals were racing—a known fast one (the hare) and a known slow one (the tortoise). The hare predictably sprinted off to a fast start. Feeling overconfident in its lead, it took a hubris-fueled nap. Meanwhile, the tortoise showed great patience, persistence, and fortitude—keeping its pace, eventually passing the hare, and winning the race.

The moral being, the thing that gets out to the fastest start isn't always the best. (See chapter 3 for another example of this moral.)

We can apply this moral when emotion overpowers reason and dictates what we say and do. We've all been there. Sending an angry email, saying something because we're feeling hurt, making decisions out of impulse and desire—only to look back and wish we'd been more thoughtful and patient.

In these moments, two key parts of our brain—the emotional brain and the rational brain—are basically in a race. Just like the tortoise and hare. The hare is our emotional brain—the one that always sprints out to a lead. The tortoise is our rational brain—the one that, if given a chance, can catch up and surpass its competitor.

It's not that the emotional brain is bad and the rational brain is good. They're both vital to our existence. It's just that the emotional brain has the evolutionary advantage over the rational brain.

The emotional brain formed first in humans (LeDoux 2012), and it's the part of our brain that kept us alive when, e.g., a predator would attack. The emotional brain would react very, very, very fast, sending our body signals to fight back, or get the hell out of there.

The rational brain formed many years later (LeDoux 2012), and it's responsible for things like language, abstract thought, learning, and impulse control—all the things we need to catch up to the emotional brain after it gets off to a fast start.

Here's the key to struggling less with the emotional brain overpowering the rational brain: using our rational brain to call out and talk to our emotional brain—thereby allowing the rational brain to have input during high-emotion times.

Calling out the emotional brain is a crucial first step here. This requires you to recognize times when your emotional brain is predominating, then saying something like, *That's my emotional brain reacting.* Or use the apt and succinct term "harebrained" to describe these moments.

Talking to the emotional brain comes next. Take your pick here, using words you know will help calm you down, connect you to the present moment, and help you to think clearly. Things like, *I'm in control, I'm catching up,* or *I just need a moment.*

If we can train our brain to detect the sprinting hare, slow it down, and allow the tortoise to catch up, then we'll struggle less with overpowering emotions. And we'll live a life based on an effective combination of reason and emotion.

How to Deal

1. Identify some past moments when your emotional reaction predominated. Maybe these were social situations, at work, or in traffic.
2. Name the emotion you felt in these moments. Label these as "emotional-brain moments," "harebrained," or something similar.

3. For each moment, generate a couple phrases that could soothe you, buy you some time, and give you access to your rational brain.
4. Compile these phrases into a list, and make the list accessible—in your phone, in your email, on a sticky note you put on your bathroom mirror, etc.
5. The next time your emotional brain takes over your rational brain, access this list. Read it out loud, enough times that you've reconnected with your rational brain and can respond to the situation more effectively.

39

Manage Your E(motion)mail

Struggle: *processing multiple emotions*

This chapter is about how to manage overwhelm due to feeling multiple emotions simultaneously.

Emotions are a lot like emails, for better or for worse. For better, both can serve positive functions: facilitating connections, communicating our inner experience, and sharing meaningful moments with others.

For worse, they both frequently pop up uninvited into our lives. Often, the sheer number of them is daunting. Many are junk or otherwise not worth responding to. Even the welcomed ones can be taxing and time-consuming to deal with.

It's taken me years to develop a system to manage emails. For starters, I *check* my email at least a few times daily. As I scan my new emails, I quickly, internally *label* them (e.g., *urgent, junk, it can wait*). I *delete* the emails that don't deserve my time—which feels amazing, lol. I then *respond to some* remaining emails, one at a time, and leave others for later. I *prevent the buildup* of emails over time, because I find the buildup stressful.

It took me a while to realize it, but this same management system can be used to manage emotions.

First, *check* on your emotions a few times daily. *Label* each emotion as you complete your check (e.g., *frustrated, excited, relieved*). *Delete* the emotions that don't deserve your attention. *Respond to some* emotions, one at a time. Save the rest for later, as long as you *prevent the buildup* of too many emotions over time.

Let's dig into each of these steps.

Check on your emotions by using two skills previously discussed: completing a check-in checklist (chapter 1) and setting an alarm (chapter 24). Your check-in checklist can include asking yourself, *What am I feeling right now?* and *What's going on in my body?* Often our physiology gives us clues to what we're feeling, e.g., heart racing = fear.

Label your emotions with good old-fashioned emotion jargon. Start with some common emotion words: "happy," "sad," "angry," "fear," "pride," "surprise." Over time, build your emotion lexicon by learning more nuanced emotion words, e.g., "envy," "contentment," "guilt," "skeptical."

Delete emotions with either self-talk, e.g., *Not now, jealousy,* or *I don't have time, guilt,* or with a dismissive noise. My friend used to replicate the sound a car makes when the driver slams on the brakes to signal to himself "stop."

Respond to emotions using another twofer: First, use self-talk that acknowledges, contextualizes, and validates—something like, *I'm feeling angry because my coworker just slighted me, and my reaction's legit.* Then, depending on the emotion, either celebrate it, sit with it, or quell it with self-soothing.

Prevent the buildup of emotions by noting any "leftover" emotions from your check-ins and revisiting them during your next *check*.

And hey, if you don't like this email system, simply unsubscribe.

How to Deal

1. Implement the system above for one or two weeks. Start with daily reminders to *check* on your emotions, and complete a check-in checklist when you get the reminder.
2. To help *label,* build your emotion vocabulary by learning some new emotion words every now and then. Additionally, you can work backward: Whenever you catch yourself feeling an emotion and you *know* what that emotion is, take a moment to register that—in case you feel the same thing in the future and want to label it more easily then.

3. Practice self-talk throughout your day when you're *not* managing emotions. This will help you use self-talk when you attempt to *delete* and *respond* to emotions.
4. Keep a log of any leftover emotions to *prevent the buildup*. This can be on your phone, in a journal, in an ongoing email thread to yourself, etc.

40

Make a To-Don't List

Struggle: repeating past mistakes

You'll have to believe me on this one: I've used skill with clients for years, before people like an uber-famous Chicago talk show host posted about it on her website. I appreciate being in good company, though.

Many of us use to-do lists in our everyday life. In fact, some of us use them as our primary organizational and motivational mechanism. They're ever-changing—filled with our current, required tasks, always being refilled by the task du jour.

A to-don't list is different in several important ways. Most obviously, it's a list of things you don't want to do versus a list of things you have to do. More substantively, it's an ever-growing list versus a list of things you hope to decrease. It's a list you review before doing something versus a list you review after completing an activity, to check it off.

And perhaps most relevant to this book, it's a list that can help you take control of your experience when you're not okay—specifically by guiding you away from past problematic patterns.

A few suggestions for making your to-don't list: First, make it compassionately, not punitively. The goal here is to make a list that helps you avoid future mistakes, instead of a list that makes you feel bad for past mistakes.

Second, be concrete and specific with your list. It'll be more useful to see, "Don't date people who insult me," compared to "Don't date jerks." That said, your to-don't list can include things other than behaviors—namely, thoughts. If you've identified that you have fortune-telling thoughts that predict you'll fail before you do something, "Don't predict my own failure" can go on your list.

Third, stay open to editing your list as you live, learn, and change. Maybe last year, "Don't stay up past midnight" was very relevant to your well-being, but this year, it's less so.

Lastly, practice compassion once again if you do something on your to-don't list. The to-don't list is meant to be aspirational, not rigidly prescriptive.

Now, let's move forward ironically by putting "make a to-don't list" on your to-do list.

How to Deal

1. Reflect on your recent past, noting if you engaged in a behavior, relationship, or cognitive or emotional pattern that you don't want to repeat.

2. Reflect on your distant past, noting the same.
3. For each thing you've generated in #1 and #2, check that it's clear and specific.
4. Create an actual list of these things—on your phone, in a notebook, in an email, etc.
5. Review this list either once every month, before any big decision, when you feel uneasy, or when you feel a negative, familiar feeling.
6. Edit and add to the list over time.
7. Consider a max number for the list—something like twenty things, tops. And consider making categories for the list, i.e., behaviors, thoughts, relationships—organizing items so they're specific to each category.

41

Write a Pre-Script

Struggle: *you shut down*

Have you ever been having a regular day, and something happens that causes you to shut down? You suddenly can't think clearly, you're overwhelmed with negative emotions, and you either see yourself as deeply flawed or the world as a dark, scary place. You feel this way for days or weeks.

One explanation for such moments is that a negative *schema* has been activated.

What's a schema? Well, imagine being a kid, and someone gives you a script to read and memorize. You read and memorize it so well, that it becomes embedded in your long-term memory. Years later, you don't think of the script actively. But, when something happens that reminds you of the script, it all comes flooding back, causing you to regress to the former version of yourself that you were when you learned the script.

A schema is like that script. Except, it's not given to you to read and memorize. Instead, it forms when something happens that makes you feel helpless, abandoned, unlovable, worthless, or rejected (Beck and Beck 2011). This deep emotional experience becomes embedded in you and sits dormant, until it's activated by something in the present.

Let's say your parents/guardians neglected you, repeatedly called you "too needy," and rarely showed you affection. This made you feel rejected and unlovable. You may have "memorized this script" and eventually formed a schema that says, *I'm too needy to be lovable.* Nowadays, if someone even casually jokes, "You're so needy!," this schema could activate.

Once a schema activates, the related script plays out, transporting you back to earlier in life when the schema formed and when you felt discombobulated and wounded. You're flooded with negative thoughts, emotions, and memories from your past. That's what leads to the shutdown.

Because schema activations can cause shutdowns, it's hard to combat them in the moment. But you can *prepare* for a schema activation and the shutdown, by preemptively writing a new script to follow during times of activation. Hence the term, "pre-script."

Having a pre-script is like having a recipe for a difficult meal to prepare. The recipe already's written; you just have to consult it when it's time to cook.

I recommend including a few things in your pre-script. Note, these recommendations are comprised of skills from previous chapters, reflecting that successfully responding to schema activations requires multiple developed skills.

First, label your current experience (chapters 12, 14, 20, 29, 38, 39) as a schema activation to orient you to what's happening. Try attuning to the present moment (chapter 10) to connect you to now, instead of being dragged back into the past.

Remind yourself of the origin of the schema to facilitate doing self-compassion (chapter 9). Relatedly, practice self-care (chapter 19) to bring joy during the dark schema-activation time.

Challenge current self-critical thoughts (chapter 35) to provide counter-evidence to the schema's negative assertions.

Seek support from community members and loved ones (chapter 31) to remind you of who you are now—a nice antidote to the schema that's pulling you into your past.

Be patient (chapter 28), because a schema activation is like a physical injury—legitimate recovery takes time.

Finally, add your own elements to your pre-script. You know yourself best, so you can include things you think/know will combat the schema shutdown.

When followed, pre-scripts can reduce the strength, duration, and frequency of schema activations, thus pulling you back into the present instead of being stuck in a version of yourself that's regressive and overwhelmed.

How to Deal

1. Identify which schema(s) you're most vulnerable to: feeling helpless, abandoned, unlovable, worthless, rejected; or other times in your life you've shut down.
2. Create an easily accessible document, email, or note on your phone for each pre-script you write.
3. Based on past experiences, current insight, and my suggestions, select five to ten strategies for each pre-script.
4. Add specifics to each strategy. For example, for challenging self-critical thoughts, generate specific thoughts you'll use to challenge self-critique: *I'm not too needy. I'm a balance of autonomous and appropriately reliant on others.*
5. Specify the order of your pre-script, how long you'll do each thing, etc.
6. Reference the pre-script repeatedly during any potential schema activation.

42

Sign Your Own Permission Slip

Struggle: *holding yourself back*

The concept of *permission* is weird. Our early life is filled with times when we must get permission from others—parents/guardians, teachers, babysitters, etc. An obvious example is needing a signed permission slip to go on field trips in school. But more frequently, we grow up needing to ask permission to speak, eat a snack, watch cartoons, go to the bathroom, date someone, stay out past curfew, etc.

I suppose this makes sense. Many of us likely wouldn't have survived childhood if we did whatever we wanted, without needing permission. But still, reflecting on this phenomenon, it's weird to have to ask to, like, pee.

Fast forward to adulthood—a time when we're supposedly independent and volitional. We get to make our own decisions: speak when we want, stay out late, watch cartoons!

The problem is, because we repeatedly had to ask for permission from others growing up, as adults, we might not have the skill set to give ourselves permission to do things.

Permission applies to not only our behaviors but also our thoughts and emotions. Clients often ask me, "Do you think it's okay if I (think X) or (feel Y)?" I'll usually bounce the question back, saying, "Well, do *you* think it's okay?" I'm trying to help them sign their own permission slip—to think, feel, and act in a way that works for them.

What does signing your own permission slip look like? First, identify something you'd like to think, feel, or do—but aren't. Maybe it's thinking *I'm fabulous,* or feeling mad at your cousin, or masturbating.

Next, think of yourself as a former teacher, creating a permission slip for your parent/guardian to sign. I recommend you actually write permission for something—on paper, in an email, or in your phone—to help concretize the process. Get specific with time here, e.g., "I, _____, give myself permission to remind myself *I'm fabulous* 10x a day", "...feel mad at my cousin whenever the feeling comes up," or "...masturbate once a week."

Then, each week or so, check in that you're doing the thing you gave yourself permission for.

Give permission for things you know support your well-being. Permitting yourself to party hard one weekend is reasonable, whereas permitting yourself to party hard every weekend may be damaging.

Finally, giving yourself permission comes with a known risk: What if you give yourself permission for something and it doesn't work out? I guess you'd have only yourself to blame—which is scary!

When this happens, we can double down on the skill—specifically, by signing a permission slip to forgive yourself for mistakes.

Signing your own permission slips can be self-affirming, liberating, and fun. Just make sure you read all the fine print!

How to Deal

1. Identify a thought, feeling, or behavior that you want to engage in but aren't.
2. Create a permission slip for yourself to do this thing, following the suggestions above.
3. Sign the permission slip.
4. Print and file the permission slip somewhere to increase the sense that it's an actual contract with yourself.
5. Do the thing you've given yourself permission for.
6. Review your signed permission slips every few months. This can be empowering and move you toward a time when you don't need permission slips anymore.

43

Take an UPR

Struggle: loving yourself

Those of us who consume caffeine may like that it's an "upper." It makes you feel stimulated, energized, and generally up. While I'm not suggesting you take any uppers, I do suggest that when you're not okay, you consider taking an UPR.

"UPR" is both an acronym and a skill that can help us deal with struggles related to self-love. UPR stands for "unconditional positive regard" (Rogers 1957).

"Unconditional" means without any condition or specific criteria you have to meet. In other words, all the time, without exception. "Positive regard" basically means thinking of yourself and treating yourself positively. Like when you do self-compassion, forgive yourself, and celebrate yourself. In most basic terms, positive regard means love. And by extension, taking a UPR means doing something specific in that moment to give yourself unconditional love.

So, UPR means treating yourself with love, no matter what.

UPR relates to self-care and self-compassion insofar as it focuses on cultivating self-love and joy. However, UPR is unique in its focus on "unconditional" self-love.

UPR is important for everyone to receive, particularly early in life from our loved ones (Sharf 2015). Receiving UPR early on teaches us we're worthy and lovable even if we're imperfect.

If we don't get enough UPR growing up, then later we may believe we're lovable, capable, and worthy only if we meet certain conditions—like being pretty, smart, masculine, feminine, young, or good enough. We may have automatic thoughts like *I need X to feel good about myself*, where X = a job, partner, high proficiency at something, a specific body type, etc.

The truth is, regardless of how much UPR you received growing up, when you're struggling to love yourself now—feeling frustrated, disappointed, embarrassed, or ashamed—*taking an UPR* will undoubtedly help.

Taking an UPR can look and sound like many things. You can say loving words to yourself, like *I deserve happiness, every day, no matter what*. You can genuinely forgive yourself for a perceived mistake. You can do something you know brings you joy, like looking up cute pictures of puppies. There's really no wrong way to take an UPR, as long as it's both unconditional and positive.

Take an UPR every day. A dose of love, without exception. A sip of acceptance, without meeting benchmarks. A hit of belief in yourself, even when you fail.

Enjoy the new practice of loving yourself every day no matter what. Think of it as taking your new daily multivitamin.

How to Deal

1. Schedule a time to take an UPR daily. Maybe at the same time each day like you'd do for a medication or vitamin.
2. To take an UPR, try:
    • Repeating statements of unconditional self-love, e.g., *I'm beautiful on the inside and out, no matter what anyone says.*
    • Thinking of a recent mistake you made and reassuring yourself that you have plenty of worth and value, despite what happened.
    • Acknowledging your shortcomings, while asserting your worth, e.g., *I may be late paying bills occasionally, but I'm still always awesome.*
    • Engaging in a known pleasurable activity for ten to twenty minutes.
3. In addition to scheduled times, any random moment you feel low or conditional self-worth, take an UPR.

44

Your Should Just Got Real

Struggle: sudden negative emotions

When you feel negative emotions suddenly, *should statements* may be the culprit.

Should statements are a type of automatic thought and cognitive distortion that ignore important context and sympathy. They dictate what you should do, what others should do, or how things should go (Beck and Beck 2011).

I'll give personal examples from my day. Earlier, I was driving home and got stuck in traffic. I had the automatic thought *People should drive better.* This quickly made me go from relatively relaxed to angry.

Right now, as I type these words, I'm having the automatic thought *This book should be perfect.* This thought makes me feel pressured, whereas I wasn't before.

Here's a coincidental one: I just tried to save this document, and my computer froze momentarily. I immediately thought, *Technology should work better,* which made me feel frustrated.

Should statements can be omnipresent because they have multiple sources. One is people in our life who've told us how things should be—a teacher saying, "This should be easier for you," or a parent saying, "Everyone should shut up and listen to me."

Another source is a set of broader variables—culture, society, the patriarchy—all of which can send messages like, "You should work harder," which could make you feel lazy. Or "You should perform better during sex," which could make you feel anxiety before, stress during, and ashamed after sex.

Should statements can bring on sudden negative emotions because they often compare you to an illusory, high standard that few can actually meet. No wonder should statements make us feel inferior, indignant, slighted by others, or all of these.

Some good news: Catching should statements may be easier than catching other cognitive distortions—because the thoughts include the telltale "should" or its cousin, "must."

And after you catch a should statement, use this skill to intervene: Switch the "should" to "could" and add a sympathetic "but..." statement.

Using examples from earlier, I could generate these new thoughts:

> People could drive better, but they're probably stressed by the traffic just like me. This book could be perfect, but that's not realistic. Technology could work better, but inevitably it glitches. You could work harder, but you want to save some energy for your family when you get home. You could perform

better during sex, but you haven't gotten any complaints.

Saying these new *could* statements can immediately relieve pressure and decrease negative feelings from the should statements. And the sympathetic "but..." statements are a form of doing self-compassion—one that reminds us of the broader situational context and that engenders sympathy for not fulfilling the should.

I could go on and on about this skill, but why should I? I think you could do well with the information you have.

How to Deal

1. For one week, try to catch should statements. Start a list of these.
2. For each should statement, switch the "should" to "could," and add a sympathetic "but..." statement.
3. To facilitate automatizing these new could statements, repeatedly say or rewrite each one.
4. After accumulating many should statements on your list, review them for potential themes—to build insight into which should statements you're vulnerable to.
5. Aim to use this skill even without the list, i.e., in your head, immediately when should statements pop up.

6. Bonus: Try using the phrase "I could..." to begin more sentences in your daily life.

45

The Taylor Swift Chapter

Struggle: *feeling pulled in two different directions*

I talk about Taylor Swift with most of my clients. Not because I'm a total Swiftie, but because she frequently sings about a common stressful experience that comes up in therapy—dialectics.

A dialectic is basically when you experience two opposite things simultaneously and try to make sense of that experience (Linehan 1993). The term comes from dialectical behavior therapy (DBT), a therapy that's rooted in CBT but is different in its emphasis on—you guessed it—dialectics.

Our lives are *filled* with dialectics—which is problematic, because dialectics can cause stress and inner conflict.

When you love your family, but their different political views anger you—that's a dialectic. When you want to do something, but know you'll regret it—another dialectic. When your new medication seems to be helping, but also comes with problematic side effects—dialectic. When you feel grief because someone died, but also relief they're not in pain anymore—total dialectic.

With dialectics, we can recognize and respond.

Recognizing we're in the middle of a dialectic can help us make sense of a situation that's otherwise hard to understand, and can generate compassion for the tug-of-war we're experiencing. Responding to a dialectic can help create a sense of control over the multifaceted situation and can move us toward resolution of the dialectical conflict.

How to respond to a dialectic is a bit meta, insofar as the response itself is an example of a dialectic: Practice both acceptance and change (Linehan 1993).

For acceptance, nonjudgmentally accept that the dialectic is occurring. Maybe, *These two opposite things are happening, and it's not my fault.*

For change, identify one—usually small—piece of the situation that you can reasonably change, and then channel your efforts to that. This change part is very tiny interventions (chapter 4), e.g., changing when or how often you do something. Using one example from above, we could say, "I'm going to limit political discussions with family to minimize how much they anger me."

For whatever dialectic you're in, using acceptance and change will likely leave you a mix of feeling accomplished and thinking you haven't done enough. That's a dialectic in itself, and that's the nature of dialectics—things rarely feel totally resolved, and you rarely feel wholly emotionally congruent.

With practice, though, you'll more easily accept dialectics for what they are. And, you'll change your dialectics in small but meaningful ways that help reduce your stress.

You'll still often not be okay, but that'll be okay. (Another dialectic!)

How to Deal

1. For one or two weeks, take note of your various dialectic experiences. This will help you to recognize when future dialectics are happening and to label them as dialectics.
2. Don't blame yourself for any dialectic. Compassionately recognize that life deals you dialectics all the time. Dialectics aren't inherently bad, and they don't indicate you did anything wrong.
3. Respond to the dialectic with a dialectic:

    a. For *acceptance,* you might say, "X is happening, and Y is happening. They're opposite, and they're happening together. This is uncomfortable, but that feeling is temporary."

    b. For *change,* examine each of the two components of the dialectic separately, brainstorming small changes you can make to each. Often, one component is a likelier candidate for change than the other.

4. **TEAPOT** on repeat with the change you select. If that initial change doesn't work, try changing a different small thing about the situation.

46

Eye Statements

Struggle: *focusing and staying present*

This skill's for when your mind is anywhere but the present moment. When you want to focus on and participate in what's going on around you, but can't.

You may have heard of the communication skill "I statements" (Eckstein and Cohen 1998)—starting your sentences with the word "I" so you don't speak for anyone else. This chapter highlights a homophonic skill, eye statements.

What I mean here is to make verbal *statements* about what your *eyes* see.

For example, if I made eye statements currently, I'd say things like, "I see a computer screen with four browser windows open. I see the cursor blinking on this document. I see my hands hitting the black keys of the keyboard. I see the gray computer on the small blue desk. I see the window behind the desk. Through the window, I see a blue sky, half-filled with white puffy clouds. I see a tall beige apartment building next door. I see the green grass surrounding it and four trees to its left."

Having literally just done this myself, I can tell you why it's useful: It can increase focus, calm, and groundedness in the present moment.

That's the point of eye statements. Whatever is distracting you in a certain moment—racing thoughts, emotional dysregulation, something sensory—this exercise can likely reduce that distraction, refocus you, and help you reconnect to the moment itself. These gains will help you experience the moment more fully and navigate the moment with more control and empowerment.

The mechanisms of action here—the reasons that we feel a change when we do this activity—are called "mindful observation" and "mindful description." Mindful observation is when you pause, choose an object to focus on, and carefully focus on it, while mindful description is when you nonjudgmentally label what you observe around you (Dekeyser et al. 2008).

Some tips for success: First, focus your eyes on something(s) that's not activating or triggering. We don't want the activity to distress you; we want the opposite.

Next, start verbalizing the things your eyes land on, one by one, aiming for specificity in your description. This requires you to focus on each object at least long enough to say it out loud, and to use more than one word to describe each thing you see.

This activity is probably best done when you're not currently engaging with someone else—unless you *think* of the things you see instead of saying them out loud.

Relatedly, you can use any sense for this skill. The name of the skill may be less aphoristic, though.

Eye hope you enjoy this one as much as eye do.

How to Deal

1. To prepare to use this skill, list a handful of moments during which you struggle to focus and be present. For example, doing work, talking on the phone, washing dishes.
2. Review this list for a few days to increase the likelihood you'll think of this skill in those moments.
3. Whenever you're in one of these moments and think to use eye statements, try it out—as long as you're not ignoring others or shirking duties.
4. Do eye statements for fifteen to sixty seconds, tops. Doing it too long may ironically take you out of the moment.
5. Afterward, try turning your attention back to the original moment. Assess whether this exercise helped you feel more focused and present in that moment.

47

The Mean-ing of Life

Struggle: *setting too many high expectations*

It's understandable that we frequently set very high expectations for ourselves. We live in a world where we're told, generally, more is better, and we should be the best. But in reality, when we strive for more, more, more—and when we aim to be the best—we set ourselves up for frequent failure.

Failure—and all the struggles that come with it—wouldn't be so common if we set more reasonable expectations for ourselves and others. The mean-ing of life skill reminds us to set moderate expectations. This helps reduce the frequency, and preempts the damaging consequences, of perceived failures.

The mean-ing of life skill is unrelated to the philosophical inquiry into why we exist—sorry! This skill gets its name from one of the other many definitions of the word "mean"—the one from arithmetic that's basically "the average."

The mean-ing of life is an action: It's when you recognize there's an expectation to be the best, and you lower that expectation—to be just okay. When your boss says, "Make this exceptional," and instead, you make it totally standard.

The mean-ing of life is also a mindset: that it's actually okay to be average. Instead of expecting the best of yourself and others, you expect mediocrity.

It can be surprisingly hard to set modest expectations and to be content with being unremarkable. Our GNATs—and specifically should statements—may tell us to do more or be better. Parents, guardians, and teachers frequently celebrate A grades, but rarely C grades. Every major sport's season culminates with the crowning of the best player or team. Social media influence is measured by number of followers, likes, and comments. Capitalism tells us to measure ourselves by things like productivity, salary, and rank. History textbooks proudly tell stories of geographic expansion instead of questioning the wanting of more land.

All of these micro- and macro-level forces work against you practicing the mean-ing of life.

That's why this book has a whole damn chapter devoted to reminding you that setting expectations to be average is great, and that actually being average is awesome.

So, try being less mean to yourself, by practicing the mean-ing of life more.

How to Deal

1. List some domains in your life where you have high expectations for yourself, e.g., at work, in school, as a parent, a romantic partner, etc.
2. For each domain, write out the specific high expectation you have for yourself.
3. Note how much you meet this expectation. Use the terms "always," "frequently," "often," "sometimes," "never." Also note how you feel when you do or don't meet this expectation.
4. Write out a more reasonable, average expectation for yourself in each domain.
5. For one week, try to meet this new, average expectation—and nothing further.
6. Note how much you meet this new average expectation (using the same scale as above) and how you feel when you do or don't meet it.

48

The Act of Faux-giveness

Struggle: *forgiving someone when you're still hurt*

Being wronged by someone we love can be one of the deepest pains we ever feel.

Nonetheless, often we're expected to forgive someone who betrayed us so we can move on with our lives and with our relationship with them—people like a romantic partner, a roommate, or a family member.

When you've been wronged by someone like this, sincerely can't forgive them yet, but want or need them in your life, you can practice the act of faux-giveness.

Faux-giveness is not simply fake forgiveness. It's living in a dialectic where you don't forgive someone for wronging you, but you also don't let their betrayal rule your life. Faux-giveness allows you to continue seeing the good in the person who wronged you and to share close moments with them—while understandably maintaining boundaries with them. Faux-giveness keeps you in the present moment but aware of the past. Faux-giveness provides moments that reconnect you to yourself despite still hurting inside.

Faux-giveness is a stepwise process that requires patience and time. Start by using *healthy compartmentalization*. Temporarily tuck away what the person did to you and then acknowledge and praise the good things the person is doing now. You can remember the bad thing they did, but it doesn't have to always be front and center.

Next, try to *take their perspective* on what happened (Bateman and Fonagy 2012). This will facilitate building empathy for where they're coming from. You can still be hurt by what they did, but you also can try to understand why they were vulnerable in the moment they hurt you.

It's also imperative to *process your emotions with people other than them*. This will free up some of the pain that's festering inside you while not directing it all toward them. Alternate this with finding times to *direct your pain toward them*. After all, it's critical to the recovery process that they know how they made you feel. Aim to make these times limited in duration (an hour at most), so you don't tax yourself too much.

As hard as it may be, *look to the future* with them and make future plans. This will help the relationship continue to generate positivity and not just be stagnant and painful. When you become more comfortable with this person, *increase your vulnerability to and time spent with them*.

Practicing faux-giveness may be a bridge to actual forgiveness. Even if it's not, faux-giveness will help you live life with someone you love, and who loves you, but who messed up.

How to Deal

1. Assess whether you fit the above criteria for fauxgiving someone else. If not, save this skill for another time.
2. If so, try to identify the negative emotion(s) you feel about the situation. Are you angry, sad, untrusting, devastated?
3. For each emotion you choose, take a baseline rating of where you're at right now using a 1 (low) to 10 (high) scale.
4. Try practicing faux-giveness for one to two weeks.
5. Take a new rating of where you're at with the emotions you picked in #2. Use that information, and also perhaps TEAPOT on repeat, to decide if you want to keep practicing faux-giveness, take a break from it, or anything in between.
6. If you proceed with faux-giveness, take intermittent ratings of your emotions to track how it's going.

49
Name Your Nasty Thoughts

Struggle: *understanding why you're self-critical*

Several chapters in this book discuss self-critical thoughts, and for good reason: It's one of the most common topics I discuss with my clients. This speaks to the universal nature of such thoughts.

This chapter encourages you to reflect on where your self-critical thoughts could have originated and to name the thoughts according to their source. This will create distance between you and your thoughts, which will help you evaluate them more objectively, respond more effectively, and reduce related emotional dysregulation.

For example, let's say your parents were mean and unsupportive growing up. Mom always said to you, "You're not that coordinated," while Dad consistently said, "You're not that smart." Later in life, these automatic thoughts—or thoughts like these—may avolitionally "pop up" in your head (Tolin 2016).

These nasty thoughts may show up at apropos times: *You're not that coordinated* when you're at the gym or playing a sport, and *You're not that smart* when you're trying to learn a new skill or take a test. Or, these thoughts may be ever-present, always lurking and showing up uninvited.

Anyway, in our example, it's easy enough to see that your parents' critical words growing up turned into your own self-critical thoughts later. This happens all the time—words from others turn into our own thoughts. It's a good phenomenon when those words from others are positive, motivational, and loving. But it's potentially damaging when those words are the opposite.

Let's continue our example by naming our thoughts accordingly. Thoughts about not being coordinated can be named "Mom" and thoughts about not being smart can be named "Dad."

Next, when you catch these thoughts popping up, you can respond with thoughts like, *There's Mom again, critiquing my coordination*, or even better, *That's my dad, not me, saying I'm not smart.* The second response gives you a bit more bang for your buck by explicitly separating yourself from the content of your self-critical thoughts.

Aside from parents/guardians, other culprits for planting negative thoughts in our head include critical teachers, bullies, and siblings; and more broadly, media, capitalism, and society. If you're unsure of the specific origin of a current self-critical thought, you can make a best guess, and name it that, e.g., "the modeling industry" or "the man."

Once you name your nasty thoughts and create distance between you and them, you'll make space for some of your own, more positive thoughts—and the positive emotions that come with them.

How to Deal

1. For the next week, write out one "nasty thought" that pops up each day.
2. For each thought, ask yourself, *Who in my life has communicated with me using words like this?* Even if you're not able to answer this question specifically, make a best guess.
3. Name that thought according to who/where you think it came from.
4. As the thought continues to pop up, respond to it using the new name you gave it, and ideally, a few extra words distancing yourself from it. For example, *That's my third-grade teacher. He never believed in me, but I do.*

50

From A to ZZZ

Struggle: *sleep*

Sleep is the foundation on which each day is built—from the time we awake (A) to sleepy time (ZZZ). If we don't get a high enough quantity or quality of sleep, our whole day can be off. If this continues for a while, we can experience severe consequences for both physical health (stroke, hypertension, obesity) and mental health (anxiety, depression, poor cognitive functioning; Carpi, Cianfarani, and Vestri 2022).

Sleep hygiene is one way to facilitate good sleep. You may recognize that second word, "hygiene"—it refers to things we do to promote or maintain health. So, sleep hygiene is things we do to promote or maintain good sleep.

Developing a routine to maintain hygiene is generally helpful. For example, many of us may have an oral hygiene routine—something like brush our teeth in the morning, avoid excess sugar intake throughout the day, and then floss and brush again at night.

This chapter encourages you to develop a sleep hygiene routine.

Sleep hygiene routines usually vary more widely than oral hygiene routines. Whereas oral hygiene necessitates that we all do many of the same things, sleep hygiene gives you the power to choose which, of the many options, to include in your personal routine.

For starters, your routine likely could include things *right before sleep*. Pre-sleep relaxation is the goal, and to get there, you could either do relaxing things or stop doing things that stress you out or amp you up. Relaxing activities include taking a warm bath/shower, meditating, deep breathing, drinking herbal tea, and listening to calm music. Potential activities to avoid include excessive screen time, caffeinated drinks, alcohol, excessive eating, and anything you know stresses you out. For example, I know if I check email before bed, I'll start thinking about those emails.

Many sleep hygiene routines also include avoiding or limiting things *throughout your day*. For example, avoiding excessive daytime napping, challenging thoughts about not being able to fall asleep later, and not exercising shortly before sleep.

It's also useful to focus on how your environment can facilitate good sleep. If possible, try to sleep in the same space each night, keep the space dark and quiet while sleeping, minimize disruptive sleeping buddies like partners and pets, and regulate the room temperature so it works for you. Unsurprisingly, what you sleep on is important. If possible, use your bed for sleep only (and maybe sex). Use a mattress that fits your body's needs, and if one doesn't, consider other options (e.g., the floor).

Final miscellaneous tips include trying to go to sleep and wake up around the same time daily, not labeling yourself things like "insomniac," and avoiding sleeping pills unless discussed with a physician. These are just a few sleep hygiene tips (Sloan et al. 1993); feel free to seek other empirically supported ones on your own.

Broadly, your sleep hygiene routine is probably like your oral hygiene routine: It's doable, it doesn't have 1,000 components, and over time, it becomes automatic.

Now that you have some foundational information on developing a sleep hygiene routine, let's see what you come up with. Developing a sleep hygiene routine can be an empowering exercise in which you create a personalized recipe for sleep success.

How to Deal

1. Rate your current sleep quantity and quality using a scale that works for you.
2. Note your goals for sleep quantity and quality. (The goal usually isn't perfection—it's small improvments from your baseline ratings in #1.)
3. Develop your own sleep hygiene routine by picking three to five total things you can do throughout your day, before sleep, or

in your sleep environment. Practice those things for one to two weeks.
4. Rerate your sleep quantity and quality.
5. Use TEAPOT on repeat with the many sleep hygiene options until you have a routine.
6. Flexibly edit your routine when needed.

51

Function and Fashion

Struggle: *unhealthy cognitive or behavioral patterns*

As a self-proclaimed fashion queen, I've learned that some garments are more *fashion*—they're made to look good. Whereas others are more *function*—they're made to serve a purpose. Over time I've come to think the best garments are both—fashion and function.

Similarly, we can use a skill that combines fashion and function to help with a common set of struggles: unhealthy patterns of thoughts or behaviors.

This chapter's skill is for those who've wanted to stop thinking or doing something, but can't. Those who keep thinking about their upcoming work deadline or about the germs on their hands, despite wanting to have more pleasant thoughts. Those who keep drinking excessively or checking their ex's socials, despite knowing it's bad. Stuff like that.

The fashion and function skill is based on two premises: We do and think everything for a reason (*function*), and it's easier to stop doing or thinking something if we replace it with something new (*fashion*).

Regarding *function:* Several psychology theories assert that things like our behaviors and thoughts each serve a function (Sharf 2015). Using the examples above, we might drink excessively because it serves the function of relaxing us. We might think excessively about an upcoming work deadline because it serves the function of making sure we don't miss the deadline.

Generally, it's important to become aware of the functions of our behaviors and thoughts. This awareness helps you understand why you often do or think something. And once you understand the why, you can address the underlying need.

If you understand you drink alcohol to relax, then you can try to practice alternative ways to relax. If you understand you're thinking about your deadline so you don't miss it, then you can set reminders about the deadline or try to meet the deadline early.

That's where fashion comes in: When you understand the why of the old behavior or thought, you can then *fashion* a new, more preferable behavior or thought to take its place. To fashion something new, you can ask yourself, "What's a healthier way to get to the place I want to be?"

You could also try imagining the opposite of your current behavior or thought to fashion a new one. If your current behavior is checking your ex's socials, you can fashion a new behavior that prevents that option, e.g., blocking them. If your current thought is *I need clean hands to avoid every germ*, you can generate the thought, *It's okay if my hands are not completely sanitized all the time. Germs are a part of life.*

Combine fashion and function to become more self-aware, creative, empowered, and happy.

How to Deal

1. Identify one current, unpleasant thought or behavior you experience repeatedly.
2. Ask, *What could be the function of that?* This may require you to look in your recent and distant past to assess what purpose the current thing may be serving.
3. Using your awareness of why you're thinking or doing the current thing, fashion a new, healthier thought or behavior that could serve the same purpose as the original.
4. Even if you don't have a great guess to answer the function question in #2, try to fashion a new thing to replace the current one. Start by imagining the opposite of your current thought or behavior.
5. Repeat the new thought or behavior many times to help it stick.

52

Write the Next Chapter

Struggle: *what to do next*

This book's introduction ended with "Whenever you're ready, turn this page of this book, right into the next chapter of your life."

I hope that, after finishing this book, it does feel like you've started a new chapter—one with deeper insight into your struggles and more skills to deal with those struggles.

Speaking of a new chapter, we have only this one left. And I'm asking you to write it.

You can use this book page, or the page of any journal/notes you've been keeping while reading this book, to write a bit about each of the following:

1. What are the most useful skills you've learned?
2. How will you continue using these skills?
3. What are your mental and physical health goals moving forward?

Answer these questions by writing as much or as little as you want. Or write something else entirely. Let this work for you.

I'm not meaning to keep any secrets as we part ways. So to share my rationale, I think this final exercise can help you feel proud and empowered; can cultivate the skill of taking brief moments to reflect on concrete, useful skills; and can encourage accountability for your future goals.

Plus, everyone loves a short book chapter, right?

It's time for you to write your own next chapter. And whatever that next chapter brings, I'll be sending support along the way.

How to Deal

1. Pause for pride with a praise phrase regarding all that you've accomplished with this book.
2. Answer the questions above, and/or write any reflections you have as you finish this book.
3. Schedule intermittent times to:
    a. use your favorite skills
    b. review other skills in the book
    c. reflect on what skills have been working for you
    d. revisit what you wrote in this last chapter
    e. do assessments like this in the future.
4. Rock on.

Acknowledgments

I know I'm listed as author of this book. But from my perspective, this endeavor is a collaboration between me and everyone in my life, past and present.

My beloved partner, family, friends; queer, fashion, plant, tennis, volleyball community members; classmates from elementary school through postdoctoral training; mentors, supervisors, and colleagues; students and clients; others with whom I've had fleeting but meaningful interactions; those who've supported me in ways I'm not aware.

Thank you all for the indelible impact you've had on my life and for the overt and covert contributions you've made to this project. I'm deeply grateful for you.

This book is by us, and it's for us.

References

Ajzen, I. 1991. "The Theory of Planned Behavior." *Organizational Behavior and Human Decision Processes* 50, no.2: 179–211.

Barlow, D.H. 2021. *Clinical Handbook of Psychological Disorders: A Step-by-Step Treatment Manual.* New York: Guilford Press.

Bateman, A.W., and P.E. Fonagy. 2012. *Handbook of Mentalizing in Mental Health Practice.* Washington, DC: American Psychiatric Publishing.

Beck, J.S., and A.T. Beck. 2011. *Cognitive Behavior Therapy: Basic and Beyond.* New York: Guilford Press.

Burnett, P.C. 1996. "Children's Self-Talk and Significant Others' Positive and Negative Statements." *Educational Psychology* 16, no.1: 57–67.

Carpi, M., C. Cianfarani, and A. Vestri. 2022. "Sleep Quality and Its Associations with Physical and Mental Health—Related Quality of Life Among University Students: A Cross-Sectional

Study." *International Journal of Environmental Research and Public Health* 19, no.5: 2874.

Corrigan, P.W., B.G. Druss, and D.A. Perlick. 2014. "The Impact of Mental Illness Stigma on Seeking and Participating in Mental Health Care." *Psychological Science in the Public Interest* 15, no.2: 37–70.

Cuijpers, P., M. Sijbrandij, S.L. Koole, G. Andersson, A.T. Beekman, and C.F. Reynolds, III. 2014. "Adding Psychotherapy to Antidepressant Medication in Depression and Anxiety Disorders: A Meta-Analysis." *Focus* 12, no.3: 347–358.

Dekeyser, M., F. Raes, M. Leijssen, S. Leysen, and D. Dewulf. 2008. "Mindfulness Skills and Interpersonal Behaviour." *Personality and Individual Differences* 44, no.5: 1235–1245.

Eckstein, D., and L. Cohen. 1998. "The Couple's Relationship Satisfaction Inventory (CRSI): 21 Points to Help Enhance and Build a Winning Relationship." *The Family Journal* 6, no.2: 155–158.

Felitti, V.J., R.F. Anda, D. Nordenberg, D.F. Williamson, A.M. Spitz, V. Edwards, and J.S. Marks. 1998. "Relationship of Childhood Abuse and Household Dysfunction to Many of the Leading Causes of Death in Adults: The Adverse Childhood Experiences (ACE) Study." *American Journal of Preventive Medicine* 14, no.4: 245–258.

Gabel, S. 1988. "The Right Hemisphere in Imagery, Hypnosis, Rapid Eye Movement Sleep, and Dreaming: Empirical Studies and Tentative Conclusions." *The Journal of Nervous and Mental Disease* 176, no.6: 323–331.

Gamble, C., and T. Coupland. 2023. "Building Relationships." In *Working with Serious Mental Illness: A Manual for Clinical Practice*, edited by C. Gamble and T. Coupland, 67. London: Elsevier.

Hayes, S.C., K.D. Strosahl, and K.G. Wilson. 2011. *Acceptance and Commitment Therapy: The Process and Practice of Mindful Change*. New York: Guilford Press.

Hughes, K., M.A. Bellis, K.A. Hardcastle, D. Sethi, A. Butchart, C. Mikton, L. Jones, and M.P. Dunne. 2017. "The Effect of Multiple Adverse Childhood Experiences on Health: A Systematic Review and Meta-Analysis." *The Lancet Public Health* 2, no.8: e356–e366.

Jakobsen, J.C., C. Gluud, and I. Kirsch. 2020. "Should Antidepressants Be Used for Major Depressive Disorder?" *BMJ Evidence-Based Medicine* 25, no.4: 130–136.

LeDoux, J.E. 2012. "Evolution of Human Emotion: A View Through Fear." *Progress in Brain Research* 195: 431–442.

Linehan, M.M. 1993. *Cognitive-Behavioral Treatment of Borderline Personality Disorder.* New York: Guilford Press.

Luoma, J.B., and S.C. Hayes. 2003. "Cognitive Defusion." In *Cognitive Behavior Therapy: Applying Empirically Supported Techniques in Your Practice*, edited by W. O'Donohue, J.E. Fisher, and S.C. Hayes, 71–78. Hoboken, NJ: Wiley.

Merrick, M.T., D.C. Ford, K.A. Ports, A.S. Guinn, J. Chen, J. Klevens et al. 2019. "Estimated Proportion of Adult Health Problems Attributable to Adverse Childhood Experiences and Implications for Prevention—25 States, 2015–2017." *MMWR: Morbidity and Mortality Weekly Report* 68, no.44: 999–1005.

Mohammad-Zadeh, L.F., L. Moses, and S.M. Gwaltney-Brant. 2008. "Serotonin: A Review."

Journal of Veterinary Pharmacology and Therapeutics 31, no.3: 187–199.

Neff, K. 2003. "Self-Compassion: An Alternative Conceptualization of a Healthy Attitude Toward Oneself." *Self and Identity* 2, no.2: 85–101.

Neff, R., and J. Fry. 2009. "Periodic Prompts and Reminders in Health Promotion and Health Behavior Interventions: Systematic Review." *Journal of Medical Internet Research* 11, no.2: e1138.

Nutt, D. 2000. "Treatment of Depression and Concomitant Anxiety." *European Neuropsychopharmacology* 10: S433 – S437.

O'Reilly, R.L., L. Bogue, and S.M. Singh. 1994. "Pharmacogenetic Response to Antidepressants in a Multicase Family with Affective Disorder." *Biological Psychiatry* 36, no.7: 467–471.

Przybylski, A.K., K. Murayama, C.R. DeHaan, and V. Gladwell. 2013. "Motivational, Emotional, and Behavioral Correlates of Fear of Missing Out." *Computers in Human Behavior* 29, no.4: 1841–1848.

Rennie, L.J., P.R. Harris, and T.L. Webb. 2014. "The Impact of Perspective in Visualizing Health-Related Behaviors: First-Person Perspective Increases Motivation to Adopt Health-Related Behaviors." *Journal of Applied Social Psychology* 44, no.12: 806–812.

Rogers, C.R. 1957. "The Necessary and Sufficient Conditions of Therapeutic Personality Change." *Journal of Consulting Psychology* 21, no.2: 95–103.

Sharf, R.S. 2015. *Theories of Psychotherapy and Counseling: Concepts and Cases*. Boston: Cengage Learning.

Sloan, E.P., P. Hauri, R. Bootzin, C. Morin, M. Stevenson, and C.M. Shapiro. 1993. "The Nuts and Bolts of Behavioral Therapy for Insomnia." *Journal of Psychosomatic Research* 37, no.1: 1–19.

Tolin, D.F. 2016. *Doing CBT: A Comprehensive Guide to Working with Behaviors, Thoughts, and Emotions*. New York: Guilford Press.

Wadlinger, H.A., and D.M. Isaacowitz. 2011. "Fixing Our Focus: Training Attention to Regulate Emotion." *Personality and Social Psychology Review* 15, no.1: 75–102.

Wolpe, J. 1990. *The Practice of Behavior Therapy.* Oxford, UK: Pergamon Press.

Woodward, H., S. Du Bois, T. Tully, S. Fraine, and A.A. Guy. 2021. "Results of a Brief, Peer-Led Intervention Pilot on Cognitive Escape Among African American Adults Living with HIV, Comorbid Serious Mental Illness, and a History of Adverse Childhood Experiences." *Journal of the Association of Nurses in AIDS Care* 32, no.4: 512–521.

Steff Du Bois, PhD, (he/they) is a clinician with their own private practice, and associate professor of psychology at the Illinois Institute of Technology (IIT). They have published over forty peer-reviewed manuscripts, presented research at numerous national and international conferences, and received multiple research grants to fund their work. After earning their doctorate from the University of Illinois at Chicago, they now lead the Du Bois Health Psychology Laboratory. There, they mentor graduate and undergraduate psychology students, and conduct health psychology research using community-based participatory research approaches to examine health behaviors, health equity, and health in romantic relationships.

Real change is possible

For more than forty-five years, New Harbinger has published proven-effective self-help books and pioneering workbooks to help readers of all ages and backgrounds improve mental health and well-being, and achieve lasting personal growth. In addition, our spirituality books offer profound guidance for deepening awareness and cultivating healing, self-discovery, and fulfillment.

Founded by psychologist Matthew McKay and Patrick Fanning, New Harbinger is proud to be an independent, employee-owned company. Our books reflect our core values of integrity, innovation, commitment, sustainability, compassion, and trust. Written by leaders in the field and recommended by therapists worldwide, New Harbinger books are practical, accessible, and provide real tools for real change.

 newharbingerpublications

MORE BOOKS from
NEW HARBINGER PUBLICATIONS

THE UNTETHERED SOUL
The Journey Beyond Yourself

BUDDHA'S BRAIN
The Practical Neuroscience of Happiness, Love, and Wisdom

PUT YOUR ANXIETY HERE
A Creative Guided Journal to Relieve Stress and Find Calm

SIMPLE WAYS TO UNWIND WITHOUT ALCOHOL
50 Tips to Drink Less and Enjoy More

THE HIGHLY SENSITIVE PERSON'S GUIDE TO DEALING WITH TOXIC PEOPLE
How to Reclaim Your Power from Narcissists and Other Manipulators

SELF-CARE FOR ADULT CHILDREN OF EMOTIONALLY IMMATURE PARENTS
Honor Your Emotions, Nurture Your Self, and Live with Confidence

newharbingerpublications
1-800-748-6273 / newharbinger.com
(VISA, MC, AMEX / prices subject to change without notice)   Follow Us

Subscribe to our email list at **newharbinger.com/subscribe**

Back Cover Material

little strategies for **big relief**

Everybody struggles. Whether you're berating yourself with negative thoughts, breaking down in tears at the grocery store, or screaming at cars in traffic—we've ALL been there. And it's okay to NOT feel okay. Fortunately, there are simple tools you can use to calm the chaos of cognitive and emotional overwhelm—and to feel better quickly. This accessible, portable pick-me-up is just what you need.

I'm Not Okay and That's Okay offers in-the-moment microskills—little strategies for big relief—to help you recognize and break unhelpful thinking patterns; cope with feelings of sadness, anger, fear, and frustration; engage in healthier behaviors; and improve your relationships. You'll also build insight into the why of it all—giving you deeper self-understanding and more control. Yes, life can be rough—but you've got this. And this fun, heartfelt guide has your back.

"A witty, funny, honest, and wildly helpful book of therapeutic gems that will fuel self-reflection, growth, compassion, and better mental health."
—Breanne Fahs, author of *Burn It Down!*

Steff Du Bois, PhD, (he/they) is a clinician in private practice, and associate professor of psychology at the Illinois Institute of Technology (IIT). They lead the Du Bois Health Psychology Laboratory, where they mentor psychology students and conduct health psychology research.

www.ingramcontent.com/pod-product-compliance
Lightning Source LLC
Chambersburg PA
CBHW011306150426
43191CB00016B/2349